Connecting with Key Decision Makers

Connecting with Key Decision Makers
Second Edition

How to Reach "Hard-to-Reach"
Businesspeople Who Can Say "Yes"

Michael H. McCann

Copyright © 2003 by Michael McCann

ISBN 0-7414-1494-5

Published by:

INFI∞ITY
PUBLISHING.COM
519 West Lancaster Avenue
Haverford, PA 19041-1413
Info@buybooksontheweb.com
www.buybooksontheweb.com
Toll-free (877) BUY BOOK
Local Phone (610) 520-2500
Fax (610) 519-0261

Printed in the United States of America

Published June 2003

Table of Contents

On the Cover:

Why dolphins?

Communication in bottlenose dolphins appears to be extensive and complex. A dolphin maintains an intricate social network that includes a few close associates, plus more casual relationships with others who come and go within a larger group.

In *Connecting with Key Decision Makers*, we explore varied modes of communication from sounds to body language and even touch ... just like dolphins.

Besides, I just like dolphins ...

Acknowledgements

An effort as massive as completing this book would not be possible without the major help of Cheryl, my wife. I would like to say thanks. Because of her, my schedule had maximum flexibility from the start of the draft to the completion of the manuscript. She was instrumental in "giving me space" and "being there" at the right times. Also, I wish to thank Robert B. Thieme, Jr., pastor of Berachah Church, Houston, Texas, for his influence on my life and his encouragement toward straight thinking.

Thanks to all those individuals who provide real-life stories I can communicate to readers. During my early professional years in Dallas, Texas, I wore down at least three pairs of dress shoes greeting and meeting decision makers that formed the foundation for this book.

Thanks to those who shared their experiences during the early years of Internet expansion when networking and marketing ideas were in upheaval. I am now able to keep the same pair of dress shoes for more than one season as a result of the Internet.

Michael McCann
The Business Café™
Raleigh, NC
(800) 335-8161; FAX: 919-844-2238
Mike@BusinessCafeOnline.com
www.BusinessCafeOnline.com

Introduction

Connecting with Key Decision Makers is time-tested and original material ready for immediate application, designed to help you to move in front of decision makers that can make a meaningful difference in your life.

My methods of reaching decision makers began in Dallas when I was in a sales position trying to reach executive-level decision makers. Imagine yourself trying to see decision makers who are:

- traveling on business outside the Dallas/Fort Worth metro
- in important meetings in the metroplex
- with their spouse for brief visits between more meetings and more travel

Talk about exasperation! I knew if I could meet with my prospects, I could gain a large percentage of new business ... enough to promote me from eating at fast food restaurants to restaurants where a flashlight is needed to read the menu in the evening. For more than 2 years, I tried the conventional methods of trying to "cut through the clutter" with a bare **minimum** of success.

One Friday afternoon when I was about to "throw in the towel," an idea came to me. This idea will be shared with you in this book. It saved my self confidence and career when I tried this new approach of using a very successful introductory letter. My manager became ecstatic and I went from "zero to hero" in 3 months.

I will do my best in this book to give you valuable information that will make your business development more profitable and enjoyable. During this time, I challenge you to be attentive because it is the **little** things – the **details** that are the secret to making these ideas work.

Every adult in the workforce has had moments of strong confidence in their capabilities and belief in their offering. The only thing missing is that glorious "yes" from the decision makers. **Connecting with Key Decision Makers** reveals secrets to reaching that *one* person, or group of people, who have the power to say "yes" or "no" to your proposals. This book is designed for an adult looking for "the next perfect employment"; a businessperson working hard to make "that big sale", or a college graduate looking for the "first big job".

I have found that other presentations on business-to-business lead generation substitute pep talk for straight talk or anecdotes for practical advice. Perhaps the authors assume that by saying over and over again, "You can do it," they can make you believe it.

I, too, believe confidence is essential. But confidence in reaching decision makers is not gained by simply wishing it to be true. It comes from experience, preparation, and having a practical, step-by-step action plan.

Proven methods for reaching the key decision maker for individuals, as well as for company wide use are given here. In addition, a valuable section on Internet marketing is included.

As we go through different processes together, remember three qualities that a decision maker will positively respond to: *flexibility, humility and objectivity.* I have been in sales to executives as well as being in upper level management. The salespeople that I wanted to see when I was in management exhibited an air of *non-threatening humility* and were *objectively interested in me as a person.* With flexibility in your approach to decision makers, you will be unbeatable.

Here is to your success in connecting with your key decision makers.

Part I

Connecting with Key Decision Makers

Chapter 1

Key Values and Issues of Decision Makers

Who are These Senior Executives?
The Executive's Job in a Nutshell is Decision Making

An executive's job is to make decisions. If a decision maker can demonstrate the ability to solve problems early in their career, they will get the nod most every time for advancement. Remember, even those who do not decide, decide.

Whether it is reaching a conclusion, making up one's mind or passing judgment, it is still a decision. People judge an executive's character, courage and determination by their ability to come to a conclusion and get it implemented. Someone who can decide what needs to be done and then does it, is someone who is admired. No one is as short lived as a key decision maker that cannot make a decision.

Surprisingly a lot of indecisiveness exists in the workforce, even at the top. The individual who cannot make a decision or cannot narrow down options will as a result stymie people and will get the company stuck. People really want to be led. Decision makers can make the mistake of being incredibly polite and holding back on determination. People want direction and decisiveness. Individuals would rather disagree with a decision than have ongoing indecisiveness. They want to give their opinion, but they want the senior-level executive to decide.

There is a myth that all executives are rational people, making rational decisions. You may think they study the hard facts and launch the right response every time. "I grew up thinking adult decisions were more black and white than they are," says one executive. In fact, executives' decisions are often based on human emotions of greed, fear, and even naiveté. Even they can be a little less business like and a little more human. "Everyone is out for themselves – including the CEO," as one executive matter of factly explained. "He may preach 'team, empowerment, pluralism,' but if he has a chance to get a $10 million bonus the year the company takes a $50 million loss, he'll take it."

The reality is, sometimes executives have their minds made up before they go through the exercise of the decision-making process. Whatever the request or situation, the answer is always no. One executive spelled it out: "I have a sign outside my door for everyone who comes in. It says, 'NO'. It saves me a lot of time. Fifty percent of the people won't ask, another large percent won't ask again, so it cuts my work load in half."

The executive's total existence is based upon decisions: He or she has to anticipate them, make them, change them, argue for or against them, correct them, delegate them, and live with them. Warren Buffet says a career boils down to "a tiny handful of very well considered decisions."

Here is the "wish list" for an effective decision maker compiled from over 495 businesspeople I surveyed during September 2000:

An Effective Executive ...

- builds group cohesiveness and pride
- lives by the highest standards of honesty and integrity
- shares information openly and willingly
- coaches to improve performance
- insists on excellence
- sets an example for others to follow
- holds subordinates accountable
- shows confidence in people
- is decisive
- has a strong sense of urgency
- earns the loyalty of employees
- is employee-centered (rather than self-centered)
- listens to subordinates
- is determined
- is available and visible to his or her staff

Now for the reality. Have you encountered the decision makers that believe they "know all there is to know about business" with nothing left in this world to learn? I sure have. I give the "know it all" individual an A+ in the game of life (A+ = Excelling In Arrogance).

What is the key that separates the effective decision makers from the ineffective decision makers in business? It is one word: Humility. Humility separates businesspeople who are celestial (a.k.a. "out in space") from those who are cerebral (a.k.a. "down-to-earth thinkers"). The truly great leaders in the game of business are individuals who realize they still have a lot to learn and are agreeable to being students for life.

Great business decisions come from proper thinking. I want to share with you some of my thoughts on the difference between decision makers who rely on emotion contrasted with decision makers whose foundation is "thinking before acting." I observe two opposing types of leadership: arrogant, insecure leaders versus humble, confident leaders.

Personal experiences and comments received from readers of my articles illustrate that **any** key decision maker can gain the respect of those employees who are supposed to be following this person. The best results desired in any company begin with the leadership's thinking.

Let me begin by providing definitions from *Webster's New World Dictionary*.

- **Arrogance** is "being full of or due to unwarranted pride and self importance; overbearing; haughty."

- **Humility** is the "absence of pride or self-assertion" (exhibited through a healthy disposition).

- **Emotion** is "any of various complex reactions with both mental and physical manifestations, as love, hate, anger, fear, etc."

Success in business begins with thought. Every person possesses the ability to think (although this function can be greatly restricted) and the ability to exhibit emotions.

In business, every executive has a choice: Emote or think! Man and woman were created in such a way that their heads are above their heart. When an executive is making business decisions, negative emotions subordinate (cancel) thinking. A decision maker can have all the "thinking" categorized as thought in their soul as to what is the correct business decision. With emotion controlling their thinking, though, their efforts will be counterproductive and fail. Emotional control of their soul blots out thinking.

Making sound business decisions depends on an executive's ability to maintain humility and the ability to think under pressure. Thinking under pressure belongs to anyone who has sufficient knowledge of the challenges involved.

In every decision, a certain degree of pressure exists. An arrogant executive never has to deal with true pressures because they are always being broken apart by false pressures (bitterness, jealousy, vindictiveness, fear...). A humble individual will have thinking as the control of their soul dictates and will only have to deal with true pressures in the marketplace (competitive product enhancement, competitor key alliance, competitor being better financed...).

Here are six key points for decision makers in all departments of a company that can help maintain thinking under pressure, leading to a winning situation:

1. Knowledge is the environment for thinking and humility is the servant of that knowledge.

2. Decision makers in business (all of us) must have the proper background in order to discern good ideas from bad ideas in the marketplace.

3. Decision makers have to have humility to "get the facts" before jumping to conclusions and walking a pirate plank. Without knowledge of a subject and humility to get an expert's advice, a decision maker becomes a "dupe" among their contemporaries.

4. Decision makers have to face reality. Arrogance is divorcement from reality. Humility is the acceptance and cooperation with reality.

5. Executives can win or lose in the marketplace from the moment they *think* about a business issue, not at the time an issue is made public. Victory in the mind first means victory later in the marketplace.

6. Arrogant businesspeople seal their own fate of eventual failure, long before the failure becomes public knowledge. An arrogant person creates his (or her) own judgment and then blames their failure on someone else (inability to accept personal responsibility).

All businesspeople associated with an arrogant decision maker share in the eventual failure of their enterprise. For example, look at companies that believe they are so large they are invincible, only to be uprooted by young, hungry upstarts that have humility. The humble will always defeat the arrogant.

The key to obtaining a decision maker's business is discipline, honor and teamwork ... with the most effective people at every category of job necessary doing their job well. Here are three steps that are key for a company's success:

1. Teamwork based on discipline
2. Discipline and Authority = enforced humility
3. Humility = key to overall company success

What Do These Executives Want From Vendors?

Each decision maker has two to three values in their business life that are their "sacred cows". Businesspeople who want to "connect" with their prospects and customers need to learn the other person's unique set of key values.

Among the key values for any businessperson can be two or more of the following:

- money consciousness
- time sensitivity
- people associations
- reliability
- loyalty to associates and customers
- integrity
- friendliness
- strong work ethic

The ability to retain an executive's business is directly tied to the respect a businessperson shows for each executive customer's key values. One businessperson may not know the balance in their personal checkbook, while another customer may be able to tell you the balances in their checkbook *and* their spouse's checkbook. An observant customer may comment how highly they value your hard work and determination to complete a project, while another customer may be out-of-town and rarely show interest in your work ethic. Diversity in key values of your individual customers adds spice to your life.

An example that I witnessed at our office illustrates the importance of knowing your prospects' key values. The following incident is completely accurate with only the names being changed.

Two businesspeople (a man and a woman) recently agreed to meet at a nice restaurant to discuss business over a relaxing lunch. Suzanne wanted to give Jim information he had asked to see before signing a telecommunications agreement. Suzanne had a big commission riding on the success of this meeting, so her manager expected Suzanne to be prepared and on time for lunch Tuesday.

Jim arrived at the restaurant at 11:30 a.m. this Tuesday morning because it is common knowledge among locals in the city that a wait list for seating at this restaurant starts at 11:40 a.m. every weekday. Confident that Suzanne would be arriving shortly, Jim asked the staff to seat him at a four-person table. Sipping ice tea and reviewing the menu, Jim began to relax.

Ten minutes later, no sign of Suzanne. The restaurant began to become crowded for seating, making Jim uncomfortable by himself at a table for four.

Ten more minutes passed without Suzanne's appearance. By this time, a line of anxious businesspeople filled the lobby waiting for a table. Jim looked at his watch. He had been patiently waiting twenty precious minutes as a prospect holding a table at a crowded restaurant in the middle of the business day.

"Enough. I can't hold a four-person table while full groups wait," Jim says. He pays for the tea, including a generous tip, thanks the staff at the restaurant and walks toward his car. As he is driving from the parking lot, he spots Suzanne walking toward the restaurant. Jim decided to stop his car and say "hello" to Suzanne to find out if there is **any** legitimate reason Suzanne was late. To his surprise, she is nonchalant about being late. In the parking lot Suzanne asks, "Are you still interested in discussing the change in your telecommunications service?" Jim politely replied, "No, thank you." Then he left.

Later in the day, Suzanne's manager, Tom (a friendly acquaintance of Jim's), called Jim to apologize for the misunderstanding at lunch and ask how their two companies could still engage in business. Jim genuinely likes Tom and Suzanne, so the two men engaged in friendly conversation.

Jim opens with, "Tom, I like you and Suzanne. I arrived at the restaurant today on time and secured a table, looking forward to conducting business with a nice person over a needed break from the office. I was embarrassed holding a table when Suzanne did not take the same interest in doing business by being on time or a few minutes early. Frankly, the lack of her time discipline causes me to wonder how she would handle our service contract with your company."

Tom responded, "Jim, I agree with what you are saying and I apologize. I have had several discussions with every member of our sales staff in identifying two to three key values of each prospect and customer. Obviously, one of **your** key values is *time*. As pleasant and professional as Suzanne is, one of **her** strengths is not *time*. Suzanne and I had a long conversation about this scenario and she would like to have another opportunity to meet with you *on time*. Can we reschedule?"

"You bet, Tom," Jim said. "Let's do the same restaurant, same time, different day." This time, Suzanne arrived early and acquired a new customer, a deeper understanding of key values and a hefty commission.

Be sure to keep these eight points in mind as a vendor ...

- Do not intentionally mislead or misrepresent. Zealously guard your integrity.

- Do not break promises or go back on your word ... be different.

- Do not waltz around. Do not put a "spin" on your company and its offerings.

- Be precise and crisp. Long-winded presentations lose business.

- Research the other company's Web site prior to your presentation to uncover your prospect's vision.

- Dress appropriately and comfortably for the meeting.

- Retain a "clipping service" to provide items of interest to senior-level executives with whom you have an appointment.

- Pay particular attention to grooming – senior-level decision makers do.

How You Can Give Executives What They Want!

Building relationships depend upon trust, communication and honesty. In the hustle of balancing profit and loss responsibilities, deadlines, pressure from above and sales contests, something happens to the credibility of many businesspeople.

Even those businesspeople who mean well can tend to forget the high ethical standards they originally set for themselves. It is easy to slip a bit. Credibility suffers when exaggerating a claim or overstating a usage or benefit of products or services.

If there is one thing that businesspeople need in order to be successful, it is credibility. This key personal trait does not take a lot of time or effort to establish – it just takes work, concentration and a lot of heart. The best time to set a straight course is at the very start of a new customer contact. Here are nine tips for building trust with key decision makers:

- **Delve into not only business needs, but also the personal makeup of a businessperson.**
  Figure out the temperament and personality involved, as well as the likely applications of your product or service.

- **Exhibit direct eye contact during personal business calls.**
  Avoid indirect glances and shiftiness.

- **Make sure that listening is more than just something you "should" be doing.**
  Be sure that listening is a constant effort on your part to probe for what your business contact is really thinking and what his or her needs really are. Be concerned and human.

- **Praise the history and marketing record of your company.**
  Present statistics or brochures indicating ethical and responsive business methods.

- **Strive to deliver a quality product or service, and in the quantity that the businessperson really needs.**
  Never oversell something, sell an inappropriate product/service, or tamper with the price you originally quoted.

- **Make sure that your after-sale integrity is top notch.**
  Inspire confidence that you will give this account the best possible follow-up service. Follow up important calls with notes summarizing your main points. Phone a short time after a complaint has been handled, or a request filled, to see how things are working out now. Follow through on any promises you have made, and describe the action taken.

- **Review what you offer regularly with decision makers.**
  You know the power of coupling your sales presentation with visual aids during the course of the interview. Put this same "one-two punch" to work for you in between calls. Do not miss a chance to review your pertinent sales points in writing. Such reviews will help you reinforce the decision maker's faith in you.

- **Keep decision makers informed.**
  Watch the business press for news of interest to prospects and customers, innovations in the field, promotions and changes in your industry. Send a note or card for personal reasons (e.g., if a customer's child is graduating from high school, story of Thanksgiving).

- **Notify decision makers if you will be away for an extended period of time.**
  Also, say who is to be contacted in your absence.

Eight Principles to Woo Top Brass ... Respect Their Principles

Senior managers have a reputation for being tough listeners and even harder negotiators. The truth is senior managers only get hard and tough when you violate their principles. Remember the following eight principles of communicating to upper management the next time you have to present to the top brass.

1. **Present with a sense of urgency.**
    Senior managers face much tougher deadlines for projects and dread the advances of their competition much more than before. To stay ahead, managers live with a strong sense of urgency. Consequently, they expect you to respect their lack of time, set clear objectives, speak concisely and get straight to the bottom line.

2. **There is no time for "nice-to-do's."**
    Nice-to-do's are secondary goals or projects. Senior managers despise having to listen to presentations about activities that do not relate directly to the primary goals and objectives of their organizations. They expect your presentation to show clearly and simply how your services will affect their business. If it does not, they will end your meeting early. Guaranteed.

3. **Do your homework.**
    Focus on the use of such open-ended questions as, "Can you tell me more about your business?" While accepted by many potential customers, senior managers are likely to meet this sort of approach with stony silence. Executives expect you to do your homework. You should

already be familiar with the company and its issues before you walk through the door.

4.   **Show them how to do more with less.**
     You should talk about how to do more with less because downsizing and re-engineering are so common. Do not give a standard speech on features and benefits to senior executives. Find out what they need and show how your service or product will specifically help them "get things done" easier, faster and cheaper than their competition.

5.   **Show them that you understand business.**
     To score with senior managers, you need to demonstrate that you know more about business than just your own products and services. Those who can talk about finance, product marketing, information management and manufacturing make a much more favorable impression than those who only talk about their own work or product. Read *Business Week, The Wall Street Journal, Financial Times, Fast Company* and other reputable business papers, trade magazines, newsletters and online services.

6.   **Keep it simple.**
     Senior managers feel suspicious and annoyed by overly complicated or self-important presentations. Overloading a presentation with too much detail will not lead to a vote of confidence, it will make senior managers think your services are going to further complicate their lives.

7.   **Make your main points obvious.**
     State the points of the discussion out loud – "The point is ..." – and do not force senior executives to draw their own conclusions. Being coy, shy or indirect often leads to a lack of closure with senior managers. They have neither the time nor the inclination to decipher your subtle innuendoes or wade through the subtext of your data and anecdotes for the truth of what you are saying. Get to the point fast and say it out loud, no matter how obvious it seems to you.

8.   **Provide specific analyses and recommendations.**
     The facts do not "speak for themselves" – especially to senior managers. They expect you to explain what the facts mean. Your interpretation of the facts should also include recommendations for action. Do not let their lofty

positions prevent you from telling them what to think and do – that is the kind of directness they respect.

Helpful Hints

- **Understand Senior Level Executives** – Take time to understand what your decision making prospects and customers face on a daily basis in order to identify with this group.

- **Try to Identify Key Motivators of Decision Makers** – Decision makers are just like everyone else ... they respond positively and negatively based on their individual frame of references to vendor contacts.

- **Pattern Your Presentation** – Develop your presentation to match senior level executives' "motivators" and then hold on for their "yes".

Chapter 2

Relating to Decision Maker's Assistants

Executive assistants are the "veins" of any organization. These people are at the organization's office day in and day out and probably know more about what is going on than they probably want to know.

In order to develop effective business relationships with executive assistants (and their decision making bosses), let us take a glimpse at their job within the organization and how it relates to people outside the organization. Once we can empathize with the position of the assistant, we can relate to this individual on a more personal and business-like manner in building profitable long-term relationships.

A Day in the Life of an Assistant ...

Assistants necessarily establish the ground rules with their key decision maker bosses first and foremost. Finding out from the executive officer they work with exactly how they want their phones to be answered in the office helps the organization's interpersonal relationships run smoother. Personally, as a manager, I like "Good morning, Mr./Ms. X's office," but some executives would rather skip the "Good morning" part. Others prefer "President's office" to the use of their names.

After an assistant has settled on a satisfactory greeting, the next important item that the assistant and the executive officer need to discuss is who is on the executive's "A" list – that is, which of the telephone callers are to be put through automatically, without questions. People on a decision maker's "A" list are usually family members, senior management staff, the company's board of directors, important outside consultants and perhaps a few friends. Then there is the "B" list, which is composed of the names of people whose calls must be returned the same day they are received; this list often includes bankers, lawyers, accountants, brokers and their personal friends.

Assistants usually have a clear understanding of the types of callers who should be referred elsewhere and those that should be handled by a key decision maker and their staff. The assistant and the executive also need to have a general agreement about what constitutes an emergency. It is one thing to be protective of an employer; it is quite another to withhold information that management may need. Many decision makers are delighted to be spared phone calls and want their assistants to screen callers thoroughly. Most assistants routinely keep a record of each call and an account of its disposition and once a day, advise their executive officer on the various calls not taken. Another method is a voice mail left by the assistant for later retrieval by the decision maker when they are in a meeting or out of the office.

It is impossible for an assistant to provide for every contingency in advance but, if the assistant and executive officer discuss the executive's accessibility in general terms, an assistant will be better able to cope with questions and problems as they arise. Some decision makers like to have open-door policies in their offices; they enjoy being available to employees and other business associates. Others rely on their assistants to shield them from the world.

Decision makers also have a message-taking style preference. Some like the traditional pink slips for phone messages; others like all calls on one sheet; others opt for somewhat more eccentric systems. Computers make sharing notes and calendars easy, as long as the manager is comfortable using a computer and can access the network. One executive I heard about liked all his messages written on post-it notes, so that he could move them around at will. This worked well most of the time, but occasionally his assistant would discover a stray phone message stuck to his back.

Virtually no executive likes to answer their own phone — too many unpleasant surprises — but many are perfectly willing to take charge of their outgoing calls, dialing the phones themselves. (This system works beautifully, provided the executive officer tells the assistant about the calls they have made or returned). Others want no part of the phoning process at all and choose for their assistants to handle the chore. It is up to the assistant to find out which category their executive officer falls into.

"May I tell him or her who is calling?....

If you ask a hundred executives what their idea of heaven is, I am sure that a substantial percentage will say, "Never having to talk on the phone again." In an ideal world, an executive would never have to take a telephone call. An assistant would handle all of them, running interference between management and the people on the other end of the phone. The fact is, a good executive assistant can handle virtually every phone call made to an executive officer. In order for the assistant to be able to handle the call, the assistant has to find out who is calling and have some idea of what the person is calling about. This is sometimes easier said than done.

After an assistant has worked for a manager for a while, they begin to recognize most of the voices calling their boss and the assistant knows enough about the business itself not to have to give everyone who calls the third degree. Until an assistant knows the ropes, screening the executive officer's calls – that is, helping the manager to avoid people they do not want to talk to and then to communicate efficiently with the rest do the calling – is quite tricky. An assistant has to start with the confidence that comes with knowing that this is part of the job and what they are getting paid to do. An assistant is not just being nosy when asking people questions. The executive assistant is being professional and efficient.

Many people save the assistant the trouble of asking who they are by identifying themselves up front. If they are not considerate enough to do so, the assistant has no choice but to ask, "Who is calling, please?" This may seem a little blunt, but it is the best way for the assistant to find out necessary information. "May I tell him (or her) who is calling, please?" is a popular version of the same thing, but the words 'tell him (or her)' create the impression that the executive officer is in. If he (or she) is not, or if he (or she) is but does not want to take the call, the assistant has dug a hole that can be awkward to climb out of.

If a caller is reluctant to tell an assistant his or her name, the assistant has every right to insist on his or her giving it to the assistant. Sometimes, assistants find it necessary to say something like, "I'm sorry, but Mr./Ms. X has specifically asked me to tell them who is on the phone before I put the call through to them. If you want to speak to him/her, you'll have to give me your name."

Once the assistant has the name of the caller, another decision has to be made. If the assistant has no idea who the caller is and does not know if the executive officer wishes to take the call, there is need to do some further investigating. Many assistants who are looking for information say something like, "What is this call in reference to?" Although this sounds stilted and a little cold, a nice opening I have heard is: "I'm sorry, Mr./Ms. X is terribly busy today, and he/she is not taking calls at the moment. Can you tell me the nature of this call?" A variation on this theme is: "I'm afraid that Mr./Ms. X has ten calls to return and then they have to go directly into a meeting. Can you just give me an idea of what it is you would like to speak to Mr./Ms. X about?"

A professional assistant will keep pushing until they have the information they need to make a decision. A self-assured assistant will let the caller know that the assistant is on their side and wants to help the caller get what he or she needs or wants from the executive officer. Somewhere along the line the assistant is bound to come across a person who is not honest about who they are or why they are calling. If and when this happens, the assistant has every right to express annoyance.

Once the assistant knows who the caller is and the reason for the call, the assistant must respond. If the assistant knows that the executive officer does not want or need to take a call, a polite excuse that sounds plausible gives the assistant some flexibility:

- "He's on another line, and there are several calls waiting";
- "She's behind closed doors," and "I don't expect to be able to speak to her for the rest of the morning";
- "She's out of the office for most of the day";
- "I'm afraid he's unavailable."

These are all trusty excuses. If an assistant can handle the call or transfer it to someone else who can, so much the better. If the assistant is not sure the executive officer wants to speak to the caller, buying some time to find out is a common tactic. When the assistant gets the caller's name and the reason for the call, then comes, "Oh, Mr. Y, please hold. I have another call." After conferring with the executive officer, the assistant can come back to Mr. Y and give him an answer.

How to Turn an Executive Assistant Into Your Ally

Assistants are human. Their primary job is to protect the decision maker's time. Despite what it might seem like, assistants do not try to get rid of ALL callers. Only those who are perceived to be time wasting "callers" with nothing of value to offer. Assistants are qualifying you by asking themselves this question:

"Does this person have anything of interest for the person who pays my salary?"

The reason callers are interrogated, screened, and turned away is they have a threatening approach to the assistant. To achieve your goal of reaching the key decision maker, you need to work with the assistant.

Here Are Eight Ways of Gaining Cooperation Between You and the Assistant...

- **Treat the Assistant, as You Will the Decision Maker.**
  You need to be as professional with the assistant as with the decision maker. This person momentarily controls your destiny. (Keep in mind that it is their job to ask you questions).

- **Give Full Identification.**
  Provide your first and last names, and your organization. It eliminates the inevitable, *"May I tell him/her who is calling?"*

- **Sound Confident.**
  Consider what you say and the way you say it. Numerous studies show you have no more than 20 seconds to make a favorable first impression. The assistant quickly forms an opinion of your perceived value in relation to the decision maker's time.

- **Build Rapport With the Assistant.**
  Treat them as a human being. People do more for you when they **like** you. Get the assistant's name and use it when you greet her/him on the next call or visit. Remember they are your first contact to reaching the decision maker.

- **Justify Your REASON for the Call.**
Every businessperson hears this question, *"What is this in reference to?"* Make a justification statement that will get you through more often.

- **Be "Generally Specific".** Talk about RESULTS – not products/services. For example, "I'm calling with the information necessary to help Mr. Buelas with his fluctuating computer needs."

- **Link Your Benefit to Speaking With the Executive Officer.** Use the words "value" and "interest". For example, "... and to determine if this would have any value for your department, I'd like to ask Ms. Parkinson a few questions."

- **Emphasize Why You Need to Speak with the Buyer on This Call** (particularly in response to *"Just send any information you have and I'll be sure that he (or she) reads it."*)

Try this response the next time you hear: *"Just send any information you have and I'll be sure that he (or she) reads it."*

> "One reason for my call **is** to get permission to send information to Mr. Reynolds. But I don't want to send information that is irrelevant and wastes his time. If I speak with him now, we'll both be in a better position to determine if this will be useful."

Here Are Three Ideas on Opening a Conversation With the Assistant...

1. "My name is Cyndi with Zulu Office Supplies. I am calling because I have worked with other manufacturers in your industry, and we have put together a system to cut down on their time and expense of buying the routine office supplies used most frequently. I would like to ask Ms. Taboo a few questions to determine if this might make sense in your business."

2. "This is Geronimo with Mighty High Flyers. Let me explain why I am calling. We work with companies such as yours that send a lot of air express parcels. We have helped them cut down on their total shipping bills, and we have

been saving them anywhere from a few dollars to a few thousand dollars. Whether or not we can do the same for you depends on several variables that I would like to discuss with Mr. Shrink."

3. "Good morning, Jill. My name is Shawn with Unisource Pictures. I have some ideas I want to share with Karen. (This can be a low-cost source of new customers for you). To determine if these make any sense in your case, I will need to ask a few questions about your marketing strategy."

Building Rapport With the Assistant....

On my first conversation with the assistant, I try to be relaxed and get to the point quickly. Talk with the assistant the same way you speak with the decision maker. Being relaxed, confident and upfront with my purpose for calling allows the assistant to be certain I am asking for the right individual in the company. Start building rapport on the phone by introducing yourself and your company. Next, explain exactly why you want to **briefly** speak with the decision maker at this time and wait for a response.

Often, the assistant you are speaking with is very knowledgeable about who in the organization makes decisions that relate to your product or service. This person can then lead you through the maze of people in their company and **refer** you … if you are clear and confident up front!

Do Not Leave a Call-Back Message on Initial Phone Calls

Take the initiative yourself. Tell the assistant YOU will call back at a specific time. The reasons? If decision makers do not know you, chances are slim you will get a call back. If they do call, THEY are in control, since you are not as prepared as if you would have called. A decision maker may also have a difficult time reaching you. Finally, you may not instantly recognize them, or remember the reason you called. Embarrassing, indeed!

Ask the Assistant to Help You Sell

- Leave Interest-Stimulating Messages. Find out when the decision maker will be available, and ask the assistant to put in the message that you will call back at that time.

- Ask the assistant to put the message where the executive officer will see it.

- Convey to the assistant to "sell" your message by speaking highly of you to the decision maker.

- Make the assistant part of the presentation by telling them almost as much information as you will give the decision maker, so there are no surprises when you are given admittance to the assistant's boss.

Meeting an Assistant in Person...

When I meet an assistant in person, my approach is to **be** myself. Something that I find that helps break the ice is to bring chocolate chip cookies as well as fruit and offer to buy them their favorite cola from the company break room. Many assistants I meet crave the respect that usually passes over them to their executive officer. Be sensitive to an assistant's schedule, personal interests and desire for snacks during the workday and you will have a partner to help you reach the key decision maker.

One relationship building technique that works well for me is to discover what the assistant likes to drink while at their desk during the day. Usually, I just ask the person directly what they like to drink while at the office, or ask a close colleague of theirs. When I leave the decision maker's office, I purchase a can or bottle of the assistant's favorite drink and mail it to them in a bright red heavy cardboard tube the same day by First-class mail. Without fail, each recipient has expressed "thanks" for taking time to think of them in this personalized and professional manner.

Getting back to the power of chocolate chip cookies, fresh fruit and colas. I brought these items to the reception area when I was trying to begin a relationship with Eastman Kodak in Dallas. I was a businessperson presented with the classic challenge of connecting with a high-level executive. At Eastman Kodak's regional headquarters in Dallas, Texas, the decision making executives are shielded behind an "army of assistants." My business survival depended on a face-to-face appointment. My challenge was how I was going to "connect".

I decided to "warm-up" the decision makers' assistants at Kodak. I knew that if I enlisted the help of trusted personnel at Kodak, the decision makers would feel comfortable investing time with me in order for me to make a convincing presentation. Over the course of the next two weeks and four visits, I began to develop a strong rapport with three assistants without revealing my ultimate intentions. Finally, during the fourth visit, one of the executive assistants, Magdalene, asked me why I was bringing chocolate chip cookies, fruit and colas at break time and being so attentive to the assistants in the lobby.

"I want to develop a long-term business relationship with you and the regional vice president, Richard. I only need five minutes to make my presentation," I responded. "Do you believe that Richard is available for a brief presentation in the lobby today?"

Magdalene by this time had gained confidence in me, so she called upstairs and learned that Richard was out of town until the following Tuesday. While still on the phone with Richard's secretary, Magdalene asked the secretary to pencil in five minutes Tuesday morning with me in the lobby. This meant victory for me … I had an appointment. I enthusiastically expressed my appreciation for the help the three assistants provided me and promised to return just prior to the time of appointment the following week with cookies, fruit, colas and professional presentation.

The following Tuesday, I arrived a few minutes early for my appointment with Richard. As Richard arrived in the lobby, he commented how highly his assistants thought of me and that is why he agreed to meet with me. I came fully prepared and provided such a compelling presentation in five minutes that Richard wanted to continue. Continued we did … for twenty minutes, culminating with one of my largest orders ever.

Richard and I continued a friendly business relationship. When I married in Dallas a year later, I sent Richard an invitation because I just wanted to let him know … no expectations beyond a simple "that's great." My wife and I were pleasantly surprised when we received a camera and a certificate for all the film we wanted for one year from Richard and the staff at Kodak as a wedding present. By the way, I still use Kodak film. Let me see ... I can use a new dishwasher about now. I think I will look into working with the decision makers at Whirlpool.

On another occasion, I began having difficulty walking into high-rise office buildings to introduce myself looking for new business. Using digital portable phone technology, I developed a highly effective technique to use right at the site of the office building. One morning I parked in the garage of a downtown office building. I had purchased a list of businesses in particular buildings in the vicinity. I also had an afternoon appointment already scheduled in one of the high-rises with one of my customers.

From the car, I called the secretaries at approximately 30 companies in a building by floor and type of company. After getting the secretary's name, I used the following approach:

"Ms. Parsons, I'm in the building visiting a customer this afternoon. What I'd like to do is introduce myself to the person responsible for business development in your organization. Who is that person?"

The most common response was, "That's my executive officer, [Ms. Bertram]. She's busy today and can't see you" – to which I responded: "What I want to do is fax [Ms. Bertram] some information as soon as we get off the phone. Then, I'd like to call back just a little later to see if she can find enough time to shake my hand and take my brochure."

I then faxed one of the appropriate testimonial letters I have stored in my computer to the prospect's office and called back soon afterward. Out of 26 calls, I got four appointments – and one same-day sale. When one prospect heard that I was calling and faxing from my car, he actually came down to see how I was doing it. He became a customer that very afternoon.

Helpful Hints

- **Treat Assistants with Respect** – This point cannot be emphasized enough. Executive assistants to decision makers often make decisions on the boss' behalf. It is just good manners to treat another person in business with respect and humility.

- **Help Assistants Perform Their Job** – Why not make another person's job less difficult and create less friction when you can consciously try to pave a smooth road ahead for business with key decision makers?

- **Enlist the Assistant as Your Co-Presenter** – Build a strong business relationship with all the assistants you come in contact with at your decision makers' company … they will put in a good word for you when you are not there.

Chapter 3

Earning Referrals

Do Not "Go-It" Alone ...

A constant flow of referrals boosts the vitality of any successful business development effort. The easiest way to grow your income is by asking present customers for contact information of like-minded businesspeople that can benefit from your product or service. If you do not ask, chances are slim you will receive. If you have a relationship of trust with a customer, you can feel comfortable asking for a referral. When you can depend on 20 percent, 40 percent, 50 percent - or more – of your business coming through referrals, your business becomes self-sustaining.

Research shows the importance of referrals. According to Paul and Sarah Edwards, authors of *Getting Business to Come to You*, up to 45 percent of most business transactions are chosen by consumers based on the recommendations of others.

Many businesspeople assume that referrals will happen by osmosis if you just do a satisfactory job for your customers. Not true! You need to take an active role.

Do not wait until the job is finished. You should discuss referrals at the beginning of your business relationship. Possible openers include, "I'm going to do the best possible work for you, and I will stand behind that work with a money-back guarantee. I hope that when we are through, I can ask you to refer me to others who may want similar success." No matter how you do it, the idea is to tell your customer what kind of people you want referred to you. Then, tell your customer how to refer those people.

Business professionals like referrals because they bring business in at little or no cost. Cold calling, on the other hand, takes an enormous amount of time for the few sales it eventually achieves. Advertising, even when narrowly focused on specific markets, is relatively inefficient. But a single referral can bring in a chain reaction of business as one satisfied customer tells others, who in turn, tells still others.

Probably the best aspect of word-of-mouth is that they bring in customers with a positive attitude, customers who trust the business because they believe their friends or business colleagues. Business is easier because the person giving the referral usually screens out skeptics automatically.

Referrals from Networking Groups

In *The World's Best-Known Marketing Secret: Building Your Business with Word-of-Mouth Marketing*, Ivan Misner describes several types of networking groups that are commonly used to generate business referrals:

- Casual-contact networks – general business groups such as chambers of commerce that allow many people from various overlapping professions;
- Strong-contact networks – groups that allow only one member per profession and that meet weekly expressly to exchange leads;
- Community-service clubs – groups like Rotary and Kiwanis, which exist primarily to serve the community but which also are a good source of referrals;
- Professional associations – groups of people in a single industry or profession, whose primary purpose is to exchange information and ideas;
- Social/business groups – dual-purpose organizations such as the Jaycees that combine business and pleasure, sometimes with emphasis on the pleasure; and,
- Women's business organizations – relatively recent networking groups paralleling the "old-boy networks" that formerly excluded females.

It is important to diversify the organizations in which you participate. If you are serious about generating business through referrals, no single group or type of networking organization will serve all your needs. Being a member of one group or type of group is not a guarantee of success. The best strategy is to select a well-rounded mix of organizations and join or attend no more

trade associations and stay in close contact with colleagues at other companies on a regular basis through phone calls, association meetings, trade magazines, etc. If your customer at Table Topics, Inc. trusts you and enjoys your relationship in business, it stands to reason that he or she would like to tell others close to them about you. Keep in mind that when a customer feels comfortable with you and enjoys your business relationship, this is an experience that your customer wants colleagues to share ... everyone bonds as a result.

If your customer trusts you in business and seems too busy to recommend others, ask your customer to provide you with a brief testimonial letter on their company stationery. Testimonials are "broadcast referrals in print." When your customer seems open to providing you with a testimonial letter, you can offer to provide them with examples of wording for two to three paragraphs that they can have printed on their stationery and simply sign. Examples of wording can include:

- "Susan's work ethic and quality of finished work make it impossible to look elsewhere."
- "As a result of your internal audit on our inventory system, we are now saving over $14,000 per month and the production manager can now catch his breath. You are welcome back anytime."
- "Michael's long-term interest in providing our company with excellent service and products has been akin to having a full-time professional on our staff without the corresponding liabilities ... everyone has won for several years now and still counting."

Here is the idea. You just have to be flexible and nimble with each customer, adjusting your level of "referral development" based on that individual customer's comfort level. One person will dedicate a couple of hours to send out typed testimonials to everyone in the company and another customer may want you to carry through on everything except their signature. When you seek referrals, personal or via letter, emphasize your value as a person to your customer and your product or service's value to the customer. By emphasizing your personal involvement and the quality of what you provide, you can relate to anybody in any industry.

Referrals are a Two-Way Street

One of the best ways to get referrals is to make referrals. The more referrals you can generate for other businesses and professionals, the more likely they will refer people to you. Are you vigilant in keeping your eyes and ears open for opportunities to make referrals to others? Do you pay attention when your customers express dissatisfaction with their current vendors?

It is important that you not make casual referrals. How a firm ultimately treats people you refer can reflect on your judgment and affect your relationship with them. If you have opportunities to make referrals to other professionals and businesses, it is important to have well-established relationships with them so you feel comfortable sending people to them.

Educating customers about what you do – what products you sell, what services you offer – is a never-ending process. An important part of the process is letting customers know what kind of referrals you need. Rest assured, I am not advocating that you become a pushy, obnoxious person. Key communication points can by carefully woven into a conversation. For example, to the question, "How's business?" You can reply, "Great! We just started working on a training manual for an exciting new customer, a privately held company with sales of $10 million. We're always looking for more customers like that."

It is important to keep an eye on whether the people to whom you make referrals try to reciprocate. If you send a number of qualified referrals and get nothing back, it may be time to move on and make referrals for people who are willing to return the favor. Before doing that, however, ask your source why they are not reciprocating. There may be a good reason. If you are not satisfied with their answer or if nothing changes, it may be time to send your referrals elsewhere.

Build a referral and testimonial file. I have letters and short comments people have provided about me in chronological order and categorized by industry type. By having information organized in this manner, anyone in my office can easily satisfy questions a prospect may have at the moment questions arise. For example, if I am out of the office and a prospect that I have been developing for months calls and wants to know "one last thing before they place an order," anyone in my office can pull a testimonial or

referral letter from our files that fits a situation similar to the one
the prospect is bringing up while the prospect is still on the phone.

Sample Referral Form

Here is a form you can customize to fit your particular software or 3-ring binder.

Referral form	
Intermediary Name:	
Date:	
Phone:	
Title:	Company:
City/State/Zip:	
Product/Service I provide to Intermediary:	
Comments:	
Referral Name:	
Phone:	
Title:	Company:
Address:	
City/State/Zip:	
Relationship to Intermediary:	
Comments:	

Helpful Hints

- Do not be afraid to ask. If your relationship with a decision maker is what it should be (trusting), the person you ask should be glad to help you advance.

- The more qualified referrals you receive, the easier and more enjoyable your business becomes. Money you save on marketing can be applied elsewhere.

- Referrals allow you to leapfrog the screening process so commonly performed on potential new vendors.

- Offer to provide the wording to a person when asking for referrals so that they may slightly adjust, print on their stationery, sign and give to you for your portfolio.

- If you are getting referrals from an individual, find ways to reciprocate with news/names of people/personal introductions that they can use.

- Build a "testimonial file" by industry type. People like to do business with like-minded businesspeople, preferably involved in their industry.

Chapter 4

Achieving Customer Loyalty

"Instead of spending millions on a CRM system that could tease out this information, companies can just ask their customers what they want."

Anonymous

Customer loyalty, customer relationship management (CRM), relationship marketing, one-to-one ... whichever term you use, it all comes down to building successful relationships to promote profitable customer behavior. A successful customer loyalty program can have significant commercial impact, delivering increased profitability, improved customer retention, incremental revenue, greater share of customer, lower cost of sale and a medium for more cost-effective marketing.

Customer loyalty, however, is not a simple isolated issue. It touches every part of the organization from the boardroom through the channels to the customer impact point. Customer loyalty means far more than simply creating points programs. It requires skills that cross every corporate function from strategic development and systems to database marketing and customer service.

If you really want customers to keep coming back, then toss out those glossy brochures from vendors looking to sell you the latest CRM software. "Customer loyalty does not stem from clever ploys to collect every conceivable piece of data from customers and then cross-sell them something they do not want," says Fred Reichheld, Boston-based Bain & Co. director emeritus, and Bain fellow who has studied customer loyalty.

In fact, the very concept of customer relationship management is misguided, Reichheld argues. Companies should not try to *manage* loyal customers. He says, "Long-standing relationships arise from trust gained over many transactions, and they are sustained by customers' belief that the company wishes to keep them around rather than drive them away."

35

"CRM is manipulation in too many cases. Companies are acting on information of customers against their interests – calling them at home at night, charging them at the highest price point [that CRM software shows they will pay]," says Reichheld, author of two books on loyalty, including *Loyalty Rules* (Harvard Business School Press, 2001). "Loyalty means listening to your partner creating mutual satisfaction."

Customer loyalty seems like a quaint notion in the Internet age, when customers can search out lower prices and defect to competitors with a mouse click. Yet Reichheld's research has found that in the faceless online market, customers yearn for trustworthiness more than ever. "Give it to them and they are yours forever," he says. That kind of loyalty is immensely valuable. Reichheld's analysis shows that a 5 percent increase in customer retention rates results in a 25 percent to 85 percent increase in profits. Customer loyalty is too central to a companies' fortunes to be left to the marketing department alone.

CRM is not altogether bad, in Reichheld's view. It is just that, too often, the standard CRM practices lead to vexation or worse from customers, not loyalty. Not many people enjoy being inundated with telephone calls and mailings from a vendor and its marketing affiliates. There is a good and virtuous use of CRM, however. "One of the best things you can do with CRM technology is find out who the valuable customers are – those who are staying, not just any customer willing to accept your offer to switch [from a competitor]," says Reichheld.

CRM data can do more than tell your marketing department what to pitch to customers. CRM software can also be used to determine which customers are worthy of a sales presentation. This may sound counterintuitive to capitalists, but loyalty is a two-way street. "Companies should try to invest only in relationships where there's the potential for long-term value," Reichheld says.

What Reichheld calls "butterflies" – customers who jump from one promotional offer to another – do not create that potential. Such customers often do not even provide short-term value. Think of credit card customers who flit from bank to bank following a succession of introductory rates. Instead, companies should invest their resources in courting "barnacles" – customers who are likely to stick around for many years, as long as they are treated right.

Once companies know who their best customers are, the real work begins – convincing them to stay forevermore. Dell Computer, for instance, uses CRM data to determine which customers have the greatest hardware needs and then provides extra value to that select group in the form of free Web portals. Although Dell garners a great deal of valuable customer information from its sales transactions, which are largely conducted via the Web, the company renounces common practices such as selling customer lists to outside vendors. Instead, Dell has set up Premier Pages for thousands of its best customers. These customized, secure Web sites allow customers to check on order status, arrange delivery dates and troubleshoot problems through Dell's help desk. Many Dell customers, who tend to be large companies, use their Premier Pages to keep track of system wide computer purchases for better asset management. "The Internet offers most businesses a rich set of possibilities for improving the customer lifetime experience, but few firms have matched Dell's initiative," Reichheld says in *Loyalty Rules.*

Companies typically gauge how well they are serving customers by getting them to fill out satisfaction surveys. There is a far more effective way to measure satisfaction, Reichheld says:

> "Rather than limit yourself to the fraction of customers willing to tell you what they think, track the percentage of customers who come back. Retention rates capture the real financial ramifications of whether or not a company is delivering high value to its customers."

Although less than 20 percent of companies track customer retention, a few use it to great effect, estimates Reichheld. USAA, a San Antonio-based insurance company, for example, has made customer retention the top metric for executive performance. USAA's budget submittals must address how they will maintain or improve customer retention. Not surprisingly, the company has one of the highest retention rates of any insurer in the world.

A second loyalty metric that you should consider instituting for your company is Reichheld's own Loyalty Acid Test, found at: http://www.loyaltyeffect.com/loyaltyrules/acidtest_overview.html, which asks customers whether a company is worthy of their loyalty. The 25 survey questions capture how loyal customers are to a particular company and why. Reichheld benchmarked the acid test with several companies that his research has identified as "loyalty leaders," including Enterprise Rent-A-Car, Harley-Davidson, Intuit, L.L. Bean, Northwestern Mutual, USAA, The Vanguard Group and SAS Institute. Overall, 70 percent of their customers said these eight companies deserved their loyalty – compared with less than 50 percent of the customers of a representative sample of all U.S. companies.

Customer loyalty comes easily to some. Take Coca-Cola®, for example. "People drink it because it is tradition – because they drank it as kids," said Gartner CRM analyst Adam Sarner. "It's not just a soft drink, it's a slice of Americana."

But for thousands of companies, the lack of a brand name means that winning customer loyalty is an uphill battle. There may be a vast gulf between the capacity of a no-name company and an industry giant to draw customer crowds. But some of the lessons learned by the monoliths have broad application. The good news is that industry experts have more than a few suggestions for taking a low key, low-tech approach to building a name, as well as a customer base.

Inspiring loyalty does not have to be an expensive, complicated operation. "A lot of companies just haven't made the extra effort to show their customers they are important," Sarner says.

In a way, it is encouraging that the current generation of consumers does not have the brand allegiance of years past. Today's customers are a fickle lot – both price conscious and demanding. Ties to tradition no longer bind them.

The rise of Amazon.com is a case in point. Rival booksellers Borders and Barnes & Noble battled for a decade to acquire prime real estate for their mega-bookstores, spending millions to promote their respective brands. Then, a company with an entirely new name comes from nowhere and turns the basic assumptions of the bookselling business upside down.

The ubiquity of the Internet taught customers that there was little advantage in sticking with a brand or business because of its convenient location or familiar name. Service became the ruling principle. In fact, much of the problem with building a customer base today, Sarner says, is that people's expectations have gotten so high that customer dissatisfaction also is on the rise.

"People still want good products, good service, dependability – all the things that would inspire loyalty," Sarner maintains. For companies willing to make the effort, it is not all that hard – or expensive – to foster a sense of loyalty.

CRM software can provide the tools to accomplish much of the grunt work, leaving the analysis and person-to-person interaction to company professionals. A company may send an e-mail to a customer – not to solicit another sale – but to ask for feedback on a recent purchase. A consumer posting comments about a product on a manufacturer's message board can receive a custom response full of useful information, instead of an automated reply offering nothing of value.

Savvy use of technology is not enough, though. A company can spend millions of dollars on a CRM system, AMR senior research analyst Louis Columbus says, "But what it comes down to is the passion employees feel towards the company and their customers." According to Columbus, the inspiration for fashioning employee-customer bonds must come from the chief executive. "He or she has to be the role model. Employees look to the CEO to see how they should react to challenges in the marketplace. If the CEO is really focused and passionate and truly cares about the customer experience, then that will permeate throughout the organization," he says.

A consumer message board is an excellent low-tech tool for encouraging a sense of community among customers and promoting brand loyalty at the same time. Message boards work better for some products than for others. A message board for an entertainment service, such as Tivo, may work better than a forum dedicated to Clorox bleach. The Clorox site uses a number of other brand loyalty tools – including tips for Clorox bottle collectors and e-mail newsletter subscriptions, to increase opportunities for customer interaction.

"People like to talk about products that have a buzz around them. It also plays to the human need to discuss opinions," Sarner says.

For many companies, message forums have turned into informal focus groups. "It's like a giant suggestion box – and a very valuable tool to find out what your customers are saying," Sarner points out.

Building Lifetime Customers

To grow your business, you need to know what customers at all stages of commitment are thinking about your firm, its products and services, and the competition. What do your customers believe you are doing right? What could you do better? What should you stop doing? How do you compare to your competitors?

The concept of customer loyalty is geared more to *behavior* than to attitude. When a customer is loyal, they exhibit purchase behavior defined as non-random purchase expressed over time by some decision-making unit. The term *non-random* is the key. A loyal customer has a specific bias about what to buy and from whom. Their purchase is not a random event. In addition, *loyalty* connotes a condition of some duration and requires that the act of purchase occur no less than twice.

Two important conditions associated with loyalty are customer retention and total share of customer. *Customer retention* describes the length of relationship with a customer. A customer retention rate is the percentage of customers who have met a specified number of repurchases over a finite period of time.

Many companies operate under the false impression that a "retained" customer is automatically a loyal customer. For example, the CEO of a growing computer hardware company boasted, "We haven't got a loyalty problem; we've retained virtually every customer we've ever sold to." But on closer inspection, the executive discovered that at least 50 percent of retained customers (those who made a minimum of one purchase annually after the initial sale) were buying add-on systems and services from competitive vendors. Retention was not the problem, but share of customer was.

A firm's *share of customer* denotes the percentage of a customer's budget spent with the firm. For example, a firm captures 100 percent, or total share of a customer, if the customer spends the entire budget for the firm's products or services with that firm. Whenever a firm's competitor captures a percentage of the customer's budget, then the firm has lost that portion, or share, of the customer.

Today's companies must manage a strange paradox: In the race to win market share and its promise of profit, a company risks (and often loses) the highest-margin customers and in doing so worsens profitability rather than improving it. A company interested in building a solid, loyal customer base uses an approach different from that of a company interested in simply building market share. Loyalty building requires the company to emphasize the value of its products or services and to show that it is interested in building a relationship with the customer. The company recognizes that its business is to build a stable customer base rather than make a single sale. This shift in emphasis is sometimes subtle, but it is necessary to create loyalty among customers and an understanding of the importance of loyal customers to the company.

The average American company loses 20 to 40 percent of its customers each year. Recognizing this pattern and its severe impact on corporate competitiveness and profitability, a business must move away from the long-accepted market share strategy to a radically different, more long-term approach to business: Building customer loyalty. This reorientation produces significant results. Through increasing the rate of customer retention by as little as a few percentage points, banks, retailers, insurance brokers, distributors, health care providers, and software manufacturers can increase their profits by 25 to 85 percent.

The rewards of loyalty are long-term and cumulative. The longer a customer remains loyal, the more profit a business can reap from this single customer. Research shows that over a cross-section of industries (credit cards, industrial laundry, auto servicing, industrial distribution), the longer a company retains a loyal customer, the more profit that customer generates. For example, the expected profits from a fourth-year customer of an auto service company are more than triple those generated by the same customer in the first year. A company can boost profits 25 to 85 percent through increasing retention by as little as 5 percent (see Figure 4.1).

Figure 4.1 Reducing Defections 5 Percent Boosts Profits 25 to 85 Percent.

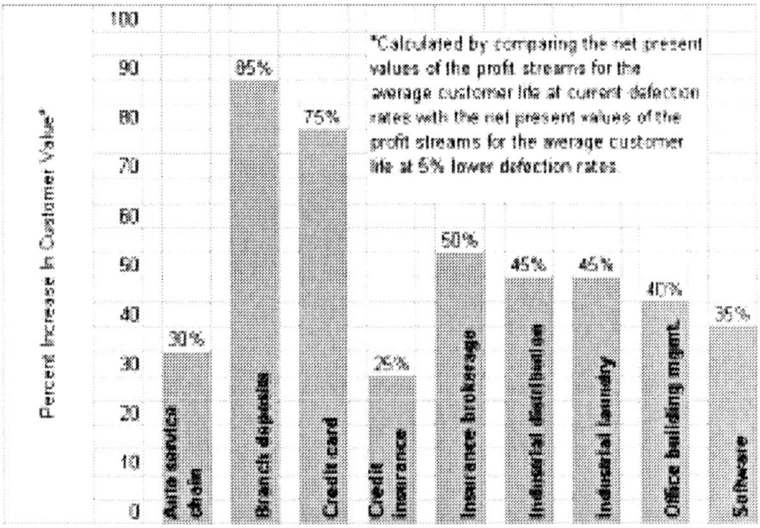

100
90
80
70
60
50
40
30
20
10
0
Percent Increase In Customer Value*
*Calculated by comparing the net present values of the profit streams for the average customer life at current defection rates with the net present values of the profit streams for the average customer life at 5% lower defection rates.
30%
Auto service chain
85%
Branch deposits
75%
Credit card
25%
Credit insurance
50%
Insurance brokerage
45%
Industrial distribution
45%
Industrial laundry
40%
Office building mgmt.
35%
Software

Source: Reichheld, F. F. and Sesser, W.E. Jr. "Zero Defections: Quality Comes to Services". Harvard Business Review, Sept.-Oct. 1990, p. 110.

If you find these profitability improvements too good to be true, consider factors that increased loyalty can bring cost savings to a company in at least six areas:

- reduced marketing costs (customer acquisition costs require more dollars);
- lower transaction costs, such as contract negotiation and order processing;
- reduced customer turnover expenses (fewer lost customers to replace);
- increased cross-selling success, leading to larger share of each customer;
- more positive word of mouth; and,
- reduced failure costs (reduction in rework, warranty claims, etc.).

But the benefits of loyalty and its effect on profitability go well beyond cost savings. As usage increases, so does profit margin. For example, credit card companies spend an average of $51 to recruit a new customer. The person uses the card slowly at first, and the profit ratio is minimal. But a second-year customer is a different matter. Provided the customer has encountered no major problems with the company, they begin to use the card regularly and more often. The balance, and therefore the profit, grows. In the following years, the customer purchases even more and profits rise again. In comparison to acquisition spending, there is less expense involved in keeping this customer, and so the original $51 investment really begins to pay off.

This trend is true across industries. For one industrial distributor, profits grew steadily the longer a customer remained with the company. At some point profits level off, but even after eighteen years with one customer the distributor found that profits from that customer were still going up.

Here are five reasons for courting a first-time customer into becoming a lifetime buyer:

- Sales go up because the customer is buying more from you.
- You strengthen your position in the marketplace when customers are buying from you instead of your competition.

- Marketing costs go down when you do not have to spend money to attract a repeat customer, since you already have this customer. In addition, as a satisfied customer, this customer tells their friends, thereby decreasing your need to advertise.
- You are better insulated from price competition because a loyal customer is less likely to be lured away by a discount of a few dollars.
- A happy customer is likely to sample your other product lines, thus helping you achieve a larger share of customer.

One other element also supports retention. When a company is spending less on acquiring new customers, it can spend money to continuously improve its product or service. This in turn can also help make customers more loyal.

Loyal Customers Translate to Loyal Employees

When a company is spending less to acquire new customers, it can afford to pay employees better. Better pay prompts a chain reaction with a host of benefits. Describing this chain reaction, Frederick Reichheld says, "Increased pay helps boost employee morale and commitment; as employees stay longer, their productivity rises and training costs fall; employees' overall job satisfaction, combined with knowledge and experience, leads to better service to customers; customers are then more inclined to stay loyal to the company; and as the best customers and employees become part of the loyalty-based system, competitors are inevitably left to survive with less desirable customers and less talented employees."

As a rule, customers are apt to become more loyal if they develop a personal relationship with salespeople. A customer who regularly buys from the same person comes to rely on that person's help in making the next purchasing decision. Salespeople also find it easier to deal with the same customer again and again rather than having to establish a new relationship. This symbiotic relationship is beneficial both to the business and to the customer. In general, a repeat customer is likely to be satisfied, and an employee who is dealing with content customers is likely to enjoy the job more, do a better job, and remain with the company. A national automotive service chain implemented a customer retention program. Within a year, the company increased its retention rate by seven percentage points and reduced mechanic turnover to a fraction of the former level.

All businesspeople recognize that training a new employee costs both time and money, and that during the training period and for a time following, the employee is not functioning at maximum efficiency. If a company is able to retain good employees, loyalty both inside and outside the company improves.

Helpful Hints

- Customer loyalty affects ALL parts of your organization and is worthy of your time to develop a workable plan.

- Strive for "share of customer", instead of "market share".

- Implementing customer loyalty programs do not have to be expensive ... the important key is senior management buy in.

- Loyal customers engender loyal employees, which engender loyal customers ... an ongoing circle tying loyal customers with loyal employees.

- It is far more economical to retain customers than acquire new customers.

- Strive to "involve" customers in your business through the use of personal employee contact and technology (Internet forums, e-mail newsletters, etc.).

Part II

Connecting Face-to-Face

Chapter 5

The Subtle Art of Face-to-Face Communication

How Communication Has Changed These Days

I say "these days" because the way we communicate – how we give and get information – has been permanently changed in the twenty-first century. Our new ingredients?

Television and the Internet

Visually transmitting information is not new. From the prehistoric cave painters to the sculptors of old who told the masses about religion before they could read, we have always found the visual image the most arresting and the most eloquent. Words, too, used to require effort. To listen and understand, to wait until the end, demanded something from the listener. In addition, the willingness to follow someone else's unique style and pace, and then to sort out the ideas and what the words really meant on one's own required effort.

That is how it *was*. But not now. Enter television and the Internet.

The two major differences between how we used to use visual information and words and how that has changed involves *passivity* and *pace*.

What Does This Have to Do With Business Communication?

You need to adapt and adopt. As a businessperson, you need to learn to offset TV and Internet information influences with inventive communication techniques of your own:

• Use what you know to become much more effective "communicators."

• Remain aware of continuing basic human needs, fulfilling the natural, as well as the conditioned, demands of any audience.

• Adopt the current technologies and other new information about visual learning to make business communication clear, convincing, involving, and persuasive.

Now let us leave the new world of TV, the Internet and other technology, and return to the original one of our *natural* functioning to explore another set of basic principles by which we exchange information and reach each other – those of verbal and non-verbal communication.

Verbal vs. Non-Verbal Communication

Picture this scene:

You are walking down the corridor at work and see your friend Ted coming toward you:

YOU: (*walking up to him, smiling*): "Hi, Ted – haven't seen you in a while. How's everything going?"

TED: (*backs away hastily, avoiding eye contact*): "Fine, fine."

YOU: "What's up? Are you okay?"

TED: (*dropping his papers, scrambling for them, getting up, and quickly looking past you as he shifts from one foot to the other*): "Yeah, sure, I'm fine. Everything's just fine."

YOU: "Gee, you seem a little distracted."

TED: (*stepping back, finally looking at you*): "No, no – believe me. I'm okay (*heaving a laugh*). Everything's – just – uh – great ... (*looking off*). Yeah, great ..."

Do you believe Ted? Would you accept what he says about everything being fine? What do you think is really going on: Just been fired? Messed up on the job? How do you know? What clues do you use to give you the answers?

Go back and review the scene again, but without the descriptions in parentheses. The words alone do not tell you what you need to know, do they? Actually, the information about how Ted really feels emerges only from what he *does*, in contrast to what he *says*. If you turned the sound off and just watched this scene, you would get a much clearer message more directly.

Multi-Messages

We all share a primary human need not just to accept what is communicated to us, but also to evaluate it. We automatically filter incoming messages through such questions as: "What does this really mean?" "Can I trust him?" "Why is she saying or doing this?" To understand fully and to put things in context, requires us to look for as much information as we can.

Go back to that scene with Ted. Look at all the information you would automatically notice, and gather from his non-verbal language, and consider how quickly you would understand its meaning.

- **Body language**
  Ted shifts his feet (cannot hold his ground). He twitches, gestures, nervously drops his papers, scrambles hastily for them (cannot stop moving, seems uncoordinated in a simple task).

- **Eye contact**
  Ted cannot look at you; he looks off, thinking. (Why does he avoid me? What is he hiding?).

- **Space relationship**
  You get closer, he backs away. (Does not want contact, avoids my personal outreach).

- **Speech rhythm**
  Ted speaks hastily (trying to get done with it); long pauses between his words (reflective, thinking of something else?); sighs as he speaks (expression of inner feeling – disappointment? Sadness?).

  And the words?

  He *says*, "Fine" ... "great." "No, no – believe me."

Words vs. Movement

Words may be the coins in circulation, but non-verbal communication (body language) is the paper money we use. Each is powerful and eloquent in different ways, but "non-verbals" have a much more direct effect on how we process information and our feelings about the speaker.

- **Words are intellectual.**
  They are symbols, requiring us to translate those symbols mentally into meaning.

- **Non-verbal body language is instinctive.**
  We absorb its meaning instinctively, through the gut, not the head. We *feel* – we do not think about what it means.

- **Words are self-edited. They are controlled.**
  Through training we pick what we say. We filter our choices through the constraints of our self-protective superego. We verbalize only what seems fitting, non-damaging, or not too revealing. Your listeners know that because we all do it.

- **Body language is not edited.**
  Posture, gesture, movement are unconscious. It is involuntary and spontaneous. And we all know that, too. That is why we use body language as our best measure – our barometer and truth teller – about what is really happening and what any communicated message really means. Remember the scene with Ted?

- **Words are specific.**
  Although words can suggest, as symbols they mean specific things and call forth the same images for all of us. "Nose" is nose. "Window" is window. "Three o'clock" says only 3:00 to everyone at once. Words explain concrete ideas and facts.

- **Body language needs interpretation.**
  Movement, posture, gesture, and space relationships are unique and highly individual, demanding interpretation. They deal with nuance, with feeling, with degree. They cannot say exactly, but they can say how you *feel* about the fact. Think of – and actually try to do – the gestures that say: "Oh, I'm late!"; or, "What, already?"; or, "Finally!"

  The gestures come to you at once? They are a little different for each of us, based on our background and who we watched growing up, but they are universally understood.

- **Words are extravagant.**
  They can eventually describe and tell, but you need to use many to get depths of feeling across.

- **Body language is succinct.**
  It shows feelings much more economically, more directly and eloquently. It evokes feeling responses in us very quickly.

- **Words separate.**
  Words are not the only difference between foreign languages and our own, but vocabulary and pronunciation define class, level of accomplishment, education, and social station.

- **Body language can unify.**
  Because life is essentially a series of universal common experiences – birth, death, marriage, children, happy, sad, hungry, fearful – we can understand each other instantly through physical expression. Need a drink in a foreign country? No problem. You will show them. And in showing them, you also show our commonality. The recognition of that unifying concept by others draws us

instantly closer – whether it is tears in Germany, or a welcoming smile at a business meeting in Dallas.

Words and movement together comprise a dual dialogue. If they *match* and are consistent with each other, they strengthen and underscore meaning. If they are inconsistent, incongruously saying two *different* things, the viewer disregards the words – the verbal – and believes the body language – the non-verbal. If you stand there *saying*, "The figures for this quarter show great strength," at the same time that you avoid eye contact, clear your throat, and shuffle your papers, you have convinced us only of what you are trying to hide!

Common Obstacles to Communication
How Decision Makers Feel About Change

New information, or information that challenges existing beliefs or systems, presents problems to any communicator. As humans, people are grounded in the familiar and in what is proven to work. Exploring is only for the few, not the many. There is only *one* Columbus, *one* Bell, and *one* Patch Adams. Even *questioning* existing beliefs feels dangerous to most people. The first reaction to change is often resistance. In order to understand what you need to overcome in order to present change at work, to bring others to accept it or wish to change anything, we will take a look at some basic obstacles to change.

Feeling of Being Threatened

The daily ongoing business of keeping up – let alone getting ahead – at work requires tremendous effort.

Status, Usefulness, Acceptance, Money push us to try to maintain some sense of security or stability at work while we gather our forces and plan our assault on the next rung or pinnacle. We climb only when we feel ready and strong enough. For someone else to move into our path and say, "It's time for a challenge now," can be threatening.

There are individual variations based on levels of skill and personal confidence, but most people think:

"I've just about figured this level out. Why do I want to change now? I can picture the present scene, but not the new one being presented. Better play it safe till I can figure it out. The devil I know is better than the devil I don't know."

So our tendency is to push against new ideas or systems, not to welcome them.

Feeling of Intimidation

Our universe needs to save face, to appear confident and competent, to seem grounded in our lives and unflappable, and this is intensified at work. That is the dangerous, get-ahead place where everyone is watching, waiting to pounce and move in or up – over you and your key decision maker prospects. Look at the concern that can be created when someone else (especially someone in charge) comes up with a new idea or imperative. We think:

"*You* dreamed it up, so *you* understand it and know how to do it and why. But *I* am not at all sure that *I* can understand it or be able to do it, especially do it well."

We think back to our early experiences in the learning game. Most people's school experience was not the greatest. We still remember the feeling of embarrassment in being found wrong or wanting in the early vulnerable days. The anxiety about our own competence does not ever leave us. Whenever you, the communicator, present a challenge to move into the "change now, because there will be a test" mode, you can call up levels of performance anxiety. Thus, the normal human instinct of self-preservation causes us, the decision makers, to put our hands up in front of our faces and say, "Whoa!"

Feeling of Competition

Your idea, not mine. That fact can create resistance again. Not only because I did not think of it, but because of the implication that you were smart enough, creative enough, even brave enough, to think of it. For many competitive people, there is also the feeling that if I accept your idea, you are ahead of me and I am in a weakened position.

Needing the Familiar

New ideas are usually presented just that way – as *new* and different. Unlike what has gone before. Bad news! This does not give the listener/decision maker any grounding or context or reason to believe he/she can tune in. We all need to feel some ownership of information before we venture forth to the unknown. Information includes knowing that past information, and experience as well as one's background, is valuable and useful in a new situation. New bytes of information create major resistance since one does not know how to listen to it, to relate to, or even imagine it.

The safest way to discuss new information is to begin with what is known. To start with the familiar and then to add the new as variations or take-offs from the old. To establish and remind one of *what is*, then show how it leads to *what could be*.

Language

Words mean instant understanding if they are used well and if they are within the decision maker's vocabulary. Since words are exact, stating facts and concepts precisely – once we know a language, we expect its words to be accurate and clear to us, making an immediate image, which is shared by everyone. We depend on processing words easily, knowing that they are the vehicles that will move us along in our comprehension. We do not expect to get stuck. We are challenged and concerned when we do. Therefore, how we use language has a great effect on how people can take in and understand us.

Effects of Not Understanding Words

• **Decision makers *stop listening*.**

The instant halt to comprehension when we hear a word we do not understand causes us to lose our concentration and the momentum built up by the communicator. We develop a furrowed brow, scanning our storehouse of language, looking for possible connotations: "Sounds like..." "In that context, it *probably* means..."

But while a decision maker does that, they have to stop listening and processing what you are saying. Then, when they tune back in again, they are out of sync and need to catch up. Meanwhile, they have missed something, perhaps the essence of what you, the businessperson, is saying. That is only the beginning of the end.

• **Decision makers *discover their ignorance*.**

The second and deeper consequence of using a word not in the decision maker's (one or many) vocabulary is the discovery that the decision maker does not know what you know.

"And if *you* know and I don't, maybe I won't be able to understand your message. Maybe there is *too* much more I don't know, that you *do* know, to allow me to get the rest of your message."

Widening the gap between you and the decision maker is a major pitfall whenever you use words to inform or persuade.

• **Decision makers learn how you feel about them.**

Even further down in the decision maker's subconscious is the idea that if *you* understand and know these words and they do not, and if you persist in using them, then you do not know much about me – your decision making prospect. You do not automatically know (if we know each other) or did not bother to find out (if you are talking to a new prospect) what I understand of your subject; that I do not know the shorthand and acronyms you are using. If you are not sensitive about that, you do not much care whether I get your message or not. If you did, you would make a greater effort to make yourself instantly clear. You would choose words that *will be* readily grasped. You will do *nothing* to get in the way of my continued attention and comprehension.

The bottom line: There are many built-in obstacles to decision makers' automatically accepting and absorbing information. This is true in general, but especially in the specific kind of information you would like to impart in the business world. You often deal with new ideas, change how things are done and try to persuade others about your point of view. Knowing how decision makers react to your business presentation is vital to planning your communications strategy.

Absorbing and understanding the basic principles of how to communicate with key decision makers – what works, what does not, and why – starts you on the road to a realistic appraisal of what you want to communicate and how you plan to communicate it.

Helpful Hints

- **Communication has Changed** – What you felt comfortable with regarding communicating with senior-level executives just five years ago is totally different today.

- **Understand Verbal vs. Non-Verbal Communications** – Senior-level executives judge you, as a vendor, more on their subjective perceptions of you than on objective data. Constantly work on, control and improve your non-verbal communication signals given to others.

- **Tailor Your Message** – Be considerate when sculpting your message to individual decision makers. Sensitivity to the senior-level decision makers' environment will go a long way toward building lasting relationships.

Chapter 6

Creating Your 30-Second Commercial

Since the early '50s, with the debut of television, peoples' attention span has been declining. Television split up programming into "segments", "bites", "parcels", etc. of information that conditioned our brains to think in terms of specific time periods. Gone are the days when a complete story is told uninterrupted until completion.

Why fight a predominant behavior when trying to communicate your business message ... adjust to today's reality. Television advertisements are commonly pieced together in 30-second increments (30 seconds, 1 minute, etc.), making a 30-second time period ideal for you to gain and hold another person's attention, possibly turning your information into their interest. To illustrate the 30-second attention span and interest, I will share an experience Heather shared with me recently.

"It took me four months before I finally got my first lead from this networking group," Heather said at one of our networking meetings. I was surprised. Four months! My first sale had come in the first meeting and nearly every meeting after that. What were we doing differently?

Heather has been a member of our networking group for about five months. Our involvement began about the same time. After recovering from Heather's surprising statement, I realized that though I met Heather at my first meeting, and everyone had a chance to give a "30-Second Commercial" at each meeting to explain their business, I had no idea what Heather did.

"What do you do," I asked her.

"Oh, everyone knows what I do," she said. "I'm in computers." Oh, well that cleared it up.

I eventually found out that Heather was a headhunter and placed technically savvy people (a.k.a. "Techies") in corporate IT positions. Heather was interested in meeting Techies and corporate human resource personnel who were interested in hiring Techies. Aaahhh. That makes more sense, doesn't it?

Heather made a classic mistake when she attended our networking meetings. She never clearly explained what she did or whom she was trying to network with, and simply assumed that because she continued to show up at meetings – even participate on the Board of the organization – that she would get business. That is simply not the way networking works. If no one knows what you do, then no one is going to give you business. In addition to the networking events you attend, think of all the occasions you have daily in order to build interest in your casual encounters.

I felt compelled to share my "30-second commercial" with Heather and describe the processes that I went through. Here is my actual wording with details following:

- "My name is Mike McCann with The Business Café," [Who You Are].

- "I am known for breaking the ice with audiences." [Attention Getting Device … people who know me will agree with this statement].

- "I am a business development trainer and syndicated columnist. My columns cover a wide variety of serious business topics with a twist of humor. Readers of my articles and books ask me to speak before groups of all sizes." [What You Do].

- "Corporate executives, Editors, and Meeting Planners work with me to connect with their audiences." [Who You Do It For].

- "Visit my Web site, www.BusinessCafeOnline.com, read my most current columns and become a Business Café newsletter subscriber." [Call to Action].

Let us now look at details to help you script your own 30-second story at your next business (and personal) encounter.

What to Say

What has to be included in those 30 seconds? There are five pieces to an effective personal commercial. Double check your commercial to make sure you have them all.

I. Who You Are – Your name and company name.

II. Attention-Getting Device

This is a way to encourage people to perk up and listen to what you have to say. Questions, quick quotes, and startling statistics are great ways to start 30-second "personal commercials." For example:

- "Do you want to make more money? I can help you do that."
- "Who here does not have cash flow problems? No one?!?! Our company can help your cash flow like a river with our wonderful payment programs."
- "Public speaking is the number one fear of Americans. Further down the list of most feared items is death. For those of you who understand why people would rather die than give a speech or you simply want to learn how to be a dynamic speaker, then we're the company for you."

III. What You Do

Make this as simple as possible.

- "We are headhunters for 'Techies' or technically-savvy people."
- "Our company specializes in graphic design and visual business communications such as logos, flyers, postcards, and other image-setting marketing pieces."
- "We are marketing consultants that magically make your business grow."

Never assume that someone knows or understands what you do because they have met you before. Be consistent with what you do. Avoid saying things like:

- "I wear several hats." We all do, but you have to make it easy for someone to understand what you do in a few moments. This type of comment confuses people.
- "My company does lots of things."
- "It's hard to explain what we do." If you cannot explain it, how is someone supposed to know what he or she can buy from you?

Now that you have gotten their attention and explained WHAT you do, you should also include WHOM you do it for.

IV. Who You Do It For

Explain simply with whom you are interested in establishing a business relationship.

- Identify your "perfect customers." This will increase the number of "appropriate" people you have responding to your networking efforts because they will know whom you are seeking.
- Who is your "target audience? "Who buys your product or service? Small businesses, corporations, women/men, high income/low income, business professionals. For example, "We specialize in Web development for companies under 100 employees." "We have programs to specifically help the elderly get their balance back and stay agile as they grow older. We use meditation techniques to help golfers stay focused and take strokes off their game."
- Are these target audiences your direct targets or is it the people they know? If it is the people they know, then state that. For example, if you are a pharmaceutical salesperson and are at a meeting of physicians, the doctors themselves would not be your target audience, but their patients are. "Our new Sneezenomore pill will help millions of people – people like your patients – control their allergies."

V. Give a "Call-to-Action"

A "call-to-action" is a simple reason for people to talk with you later. Here are some examples:

- "See me after this meeting to schedule your 20-minute complimentary coaching session."
- "Be sure to give me your business card to receive our quarterly newsletter full of marketing and communications ideas for your business."
- "Get an autographed edition of *Connecting with Key Decision Makers* if you buy it at today's meeting."
- "If you help us place an 'Executive Business Program' at one of our American locations, you are entitled to an all expense-paid trip for two to our resort."

How to Say It

1. Position
- Stand to gain control and respect
- Move to a spot so that no one (or almost no one) is staring at your back
- Use 'open' gestures (wide open arms, arms not folded across chest)
- Smile
- Make eye contact

2. Voice
- Speak loud enough for all to hear (especially when there is noise from food service or nearby meeting rooms).
- Speak slowly (especially when giving your name, company name and "call-to-action").
- Sound passionate about what you are talking about. If you are not excited by what you do, why would anyone else be interested in working with you?

Tricks to Stand Out and Be Remembered

1. Use memory tricks so people remember your name.
   - Similes: "My name is Mardi Maraschino – like the cherry." (from the movie *Grease*)

- Acronyms: "We are BABB Insurance Company. BABB stands for 'Biggest and Best Brokers.'"
- Monikers: "I'm a professional business humorist, better known as 'Mr. Business-Lite.'"

2. Professionalism – do you reflect the type of customer you want to attract?

3. Attire:
   - Colors – wear unusual or noticeable colors – especially colors that reflect your company colors. Since blue is one of my company colors, I use it in all my marketing materials and am sure to always have the color around me. During the colder months, I wear a blue scarf. In the summer, I wear blue slacks or blue shirts.
   - Accessories – wear unusual or noticeable accessories such as a dramatic hat, a striking lapel pin, a wild tie, a small flower in your lapel, a colorful scarf, crazy earrings, etc. Try to be consistent with your wild accessory so people remember you and the accessory connection.

I encouraged Heather to clearly explain what she did during her 30-second commercial. She began by saying, "Someone here told me that they didn't know what I do and that I should explain myself better. I match up computer programmers and other "techies" with employers who are looking to hire technologically savvy people. Most of you would not fit into the type of person I am looking for, but you may know a family member, friend or customer who is a "techie" or is looking to hire one. My cards are on the display table in the back. Please take one and contact me or forward my name to anyone who fits the description of the people I am looking for."

People began nodding their heads as if to say, "Oh! THAT's what you do." Heather left the meeting with several leads that day.

Now that you know what to say, how to say it, who to say it to, and how to be remembered at business encounters, you should be able to close the gap on your next "chance encounter." Get out there and make the most of your 30 seconds.

Helpful Hints

- In developing your description, address these issues for your listeners: Who You Are, Attention Getting Device Relating to Your Occupation, What You Do, Who You Do it For, Call to Action.

- Keep your memorized discourse to no more than 30 seconds.

- Make sure your description is interesting.

- Rehearse your body language and voice inflections before your first performance.

- Create "tie-ins" to your description with word and clothing choices.

Chapter 7

Reach Out at Your Next Trade Show

Trade Shows

Trade show participation can be a blessing or a curse for you and your company. The most common comment I hear from trade show exhibitors goes something like this: "Our company went to that ?@!x* trade show again this year and did not achieve the results we expected. What are we doing wrong?"

Exhibit for a reason – with multiple shows to choose from, be sure to exhibit only at those that serve a specific goal within your marketing strategy, such as ...

... image building
... a product introduction
... sales lead generation
... investigation of a potential market

Once you decide to participate in a trade show, you need to develop a complete exhibit plan to include every activity relating to the particular show. Begin your detailed plan months in advance to maximize your productivity. Participating in trade shows is hard work. Months before the "big event" you need to earnestly begin planning a myriad of details covering two different directions. The first direction involves choosing travel methods, making reservations at the hotel, signing trade show management documentation and other key logistical decisions. The second half of pre-show planning involves judgment issues such as the selection of the right personnel to attend, training these people, what to wear, and messages to send to prospects and customers.

In this chapter, I want to focus on the interpersonal relationships surrounding the face-to-face and virtual trade show experience. From experiences in attending and exhibiting at diverse events, I go through these five interpersonal processes with each show:

- Planning for literature and communiqués to communicate with my target audience prior to the show.

- Selecting the right mix of personnel to represent my company, including their training and scheduling at different show events.

- Deciding what activities to participate in at the show.

- Coordinating "who to see" and what I want to accomplish as a result of meeting with each person.

- Assigning follow-up activities to implement immediately after the show.

Before the Show

Three months before the show, I write a small, personal business letter to all my prospects and customers whom I most want to see. I encourage letter recipients to schedule an appointment with me so I can devote my full attention to each person at a specific time at the trade show. I follow up my letter within three days from the time my prospects and customers should have received them to make an appointment. Every three weeks prior to the show, I call each recipient to keep in touch.

What about literature?

Brochures, flyers and sales collateral are an integral part of any trade show. I believe literature that is displayed in view of the public on the exhibit table is a CRUTCH. Show attendees have a myriad of reasons for accumulating literature from table to table. Some attendees take the literature back to their offices to show their office mates how much activity they recently endured, although they forget to mention the hospitality suites. Other show participants pick up literature to silence an exhibitor who is obnoxious. Over twenty-five years, I have never seen a valid reason for having literature displayed for the casual passerby to pick up. I am at this trade show to SELL, SELL and SELL. I keep **all** literature out of sight until I have fully qualified each prospect.

My suggestion is to **customize** literature for the trade show you are attending with professional flyers, displaying the trade show name and dates, along with a set of special offerings valid for up to 30 days after the show ends. On one side of this promotional piece, I write a one-page anecdote on how a customer of mine used the product or service I am offering to help solve a problem with which the trade show attendee can readily identify. Map out five or six of your customers target industries with corresponding stories on one side to match each group at the show.

Increasingly, attendees are visiting a Web site after the show to avoid the sales pitch. If that is the case, distribute business cards with just a name and a Web site address only. It replaces the expensive brochure and research shows that recipients of the card are much more likely to visit the Web site because of the curiosity factor.

Consider customizing your Web site for each trade show. It is an effective strategy for products with multiple applications. Gore, the makers of Gortex, has a Gore Military Fabric site for the specific niche visitor (http://www.goremilitary.com).

For show attendees who do not fit comfortably in a category matching the literature you prepare, make a note on the back of the prospect's business card or your custom lead form with details about information to send immediately after the show. At the close of every exhibit day, fax a list of the day's prospects to an administrative assistant at your office. The assistant can prepare a personalized note for people expressing your appreciation for their interest at the show. The day you return home, personally sign each letter and immediately mail with any appropriate literature. Follow up with a phone call three days after the prospect should have received your information in the mail and decide whether to give the person a strong or weak prospect rating in your contact software.

The Right Personnel

Each exhibitor should have a minimum of four company employees at each trade show. Two of these four or more employees should be very knowledgeable about company capabilities, preferably management-level employees. You need **at least** four people on the exhibit staff because a minimum of two need to be in the booth at all times, with backup. All your team members need to be:

- **Perceptive** in order to be capable of picking up on many different verbal and nonverbal behaviors.

- **Knowledgeable about company products AND services** because each company has a combination of products and services. At trade shows, you encounter prospects that demand the complete range of knowledge from representatives.

- **Extraordinary listeners** because activity at shows moves very rapidly and you have no more than five minutes with one person unless they have an appointment, or the visitor is an extraordinarily valuable customer.

Evaluate your present customer and prospect personality characteristics and try to match these characteristics in your exhibit staff. Your target market personnel will be attracted to people who are much like them. Staffing considerations should be sensitive to types of prospects, diverse personalities and a good mix of gender balance.

What is the breakdown of upper-level executives such as presidents, general managers, and vice presidents? What is the breakdown of "end user" attendees, such as department heads, plant managers, and supervisors? Senior staff personnel, such as purchasing agents, engineers and others who specify or recommend purchases may be in force in the exhibit hall. Each of these groups will look at what you offer from their own perspective. You need to have the mix of skills in your exhibit staff to match those of the expected visitors.

Have a healthy mix of extroverted and introverted personnel in the booth at the same time to balance the attitude mix. More and more women are influencing buying decisions so it is important to have close to a 50/50 ratio of men and women.

Now you can understand why it is important to begin planning for even local trade shows months in advance. Having a healthy mixture of ages, sexes, races, technical backgrounds and personalities manning your booth will attract attendees to your exhibit. My tried-and-true method of staffing my exhibit for the "success level" is to always have one person available to greet and talk with the next person that walks into the booth space. At least one person in your booth needs to be VERY knowledgeable about all products and services your company provides. Other personnel in the booth can "funnel" incoming attendees to the "knowledgeable ones" as smoothly as possible.

One company representative needs to stand outside the booth in the aisle engaging people as they approach your exhibit. This company representative needs to be an extrovert who "steers" interested attendees to the next "available" person at your booth. A fourth, preferably management-level company representative, is constantly circulating the trade show hall mingling with people and encouraging individuals to stop at your company booth. The fourth individual acts as a "floater." This person relieves one of the first three when a rest period is needed.

Once you have chosen a team to staff your exhibit, conduct a show training session to ensure that show participants are aware of the skills necessary. A professional trainer or upper-level executive in your company is an excellent choice for presenting this class. In this class, emphasize:

- Why you choose to participate in this show and what you expect to gain.

- What products and services you are promoting at the show. You want all company representatives to have plenty of advance time to prepare with product and service knowledge.

- Goals and objectives from an individual and group basis. Trade shows are a **working** session where participants can also enjoy themselves as a side benefit.

- Productivity and effectiveness on the trade show floor. Train employees how to present company products and services and what is appropriate behavior to attract profitable prospects and customers.

During the Show

From the opening of the trade show to when the last exhibit is boxed up, you and other company representatives are like actors on stage. The attendees, like an audience, are present to see your performance. Just as you expect to receive first-class performances when you make an effort to attend a show, so attendees to your trade show expect an A-plus performance from your company's team.

Stand up straight! – three or four days behind a trade show booth is a grueling experience, but do not forget the importance of body language. To avoid appearing stiff and unapproachable, do not cross your arms or stand with your hands in your pockets. Some experts suggest you hold a pen or paper, stand to one side of the booth and view the aisle at an angle to seem less imposing.

The leader of the company team needs to make a concerted effort to meet with all the people taking part in the exhibit at the beginning and at the end of the day to keep everyone heading in the same direction. Remind participants of what needs to be accomplished, evaluating overall performance, reiterating goals and providing daily encouragement.

Be certain to get the same amount of sleep to which you are accustomed. Even if you go to hospitality suites and hotel plazas in the evening, get to bed as close to your regular time as possible. I am a veteran of pushing the nighttime entertainment too far and I can definitely tell you maintaining your regular schedule is important because you need to be alert at all times when you are in public. Lack of sleep causes your performance to suffer. Your mind and body will be dull until you catch up on sleep.

When arranging your booth, put tables and chairs to the back or side of the exhibit space. You need to open up the space to be more inviting to prospects and customers. Literature should be under tables or out of sight to encourage staffers to quickly qualify prospects and give literature only to qualified visitors or move on to another attendee.

Make your visuals multifunctional – in designing the booth, it is logical to use big colorful photos to attract attention, but think beyond that use. Well chosen photos or drawings of new products, charts of "before-and-after" processes, and graphs of results can draw the eye initially, then serve as visual aids during your booth presentation.

When visitors are approaching, show them that you are receptive by facing their direction. Face the aisle whenever you are not engaged in conversation with a prospect or customer. When the attendee is approaching you, offer a welcoming handshake. In the United States, it is acceptable for either a man or woman to extend a hand. While you are in the exhibit, be alert, active and interested in conducting business. Body language shouts louder than any other form of communication to attendees. Hold a relaxed stance to appear more approachable. Stand with both of your arms by your side. Do not cross your arms or put your hands in your pockets because this action tells visitors that you are not genuinely interested in opening conversation. When you encounter a visitor with arms that are not accessible for a handshake, offer them your business card to encourage them to extend their hand. Some visitors hold their hands close to their body because they are too shy to initiate a handshake.

Incidentally, time is precious. Roughly 60 percent of prospects will not wait longer than one minute for a company representative's attention at a trade show exhibit, and 28 percent will wait up to three minutes. Only 14 percent will wait up to five minutes.

You want to match your behavior in posture and speech to the behavior of your prospect. Ask confident people direct, open-ended questions. Ask attendees who appear uncertain only casual, conversational type questions until they begin to warm up. Sit down in your exhibit only if you are conducting serious business transactions with a show attendee. When you are sitting down, the perception to others is that you are "out of action" and not available. If you must sit down, do so out of sight from your exhibit.

Make sure to arrive at your exhibit 15 minutes before your scheduled time to catch up on the latest news from your colleagues and get psychologically prepared to be "on stage." Plan to stay at the booth 15 minutes after your shift to finish paperwork or conclude a face-to-face meeting. You should make it a first priority to serve in the company exhibit.

When you are inside your exhibit, guard against complacency at all times. If the aisles in the convention hall are sparsely populated, this is the time that your best prospect, and future customer, is likely to show up. Serious prospects of yours know the quiet times are best to have quality time to evaluate your company and find out about your company's personnel on a more intimate level.

When you are not working at your exhibit, visit the breakout sessions to learn what is important to attendees. Being able to reference a recent session with a prospect will give you instant rapport and credibility.

Bring two sets of clothing: Comfortable business attire to wear during your exhibit hours and casual wear to relax in. Business attire communicates a business purpose. Remember you are at this trade show to SELL. Dressing in a professional manner tells your prospects and customers that you are proud of the company for whom you work. Wear shoes that are professional looking and already "broken in" because exhibit halls usually consist of concrete flooring covered with a thin veneer of inexpensive carpeting. Women should wear low heels. Dress casually. Dress should be bright and business casual. Long-sleeve shirts with company logos have replaced business suits, which can look more intimidating, but avoid golf shirts. Research shows they are too casual and reduce credibility.

In order to stay hydrated, drink plenty of water rather than coffee, tea or soft drinks. Eat well-balanced meals low in sugar, caffeine and salt to keep your energy level at a constant level for longer time periods. Avoid alcohol at all times during exhibit hours and keep it to a minimum after hours. As soon as you can possibly stop by a grocery store in the vicinity of your hotel, buy an ample supply of your favorite bottled water and carry it everywhere with you to keep your throat lubricated. I keep water cool in the hotel room refrigerator.

Wear your name badge on the upper right side of your clothing. When you shake hands with your prospect, the individual will be looking directly at your name. Placing the name badge high on your clothing allows people wearing bifocals to see your name without having to move their face up or down to focus.

When you begin conversing with likely prospects, use the first few minutes to "qualify" the individual before you invest more time in a full discussion about your company and its offerings. If the prospect is not a good match for what your company offers, politely excuse yourself as soon as possible and start over again with a new prospect. During the first five minutes of conversation, introduce sales closing statements several times. Again, the objective of the trade show is to SELL.

When meeting a prospect, the first fifteen seconds makes or breaks the future, so take notes. You will meet so many people and be exposed to so many new stimuli during the show that the best memory just will not suffice. Writing while you are having a conversation with the prospect shows the attendee that you are paying attention and listening. You will also have a written record of your conversation in every meeting.

I always ask for the person's business card. If they do not have a business card, I have a pre-printed lead form on 3"x 5" cards that are easy to store in my shirt pocket (10 at one time). For a woman, have cards in a skirt or suit jacket pocket. Four key answers to capture on their business card or your lead form about each prospect include:

1. The prospect's name, address and phone number and what the prospect's responsibility is at their company.

2. What does this person want from me and how soon do they need what I offer? This information will give you the opportunity to assign a priority (A, B or C) to each prospect for follow-up. Be sure to follow-up on a specific day and time that you both agree upon at this meeting.

3. What information strikes you about this person that you can bring up again during a follow-up call to develop instant rapport?

4. Ask your prospect if they want a complimentary subscription to your e-mail newsletter. If "yes," be sure to get their e-mail address and add them to your distribution list. Also include this person in your holiday note program at major holidays to keep in touch.

Ask for more names. Identify other people with whom booth visitors will share information once they return home. Sixty percent of visitors will share information with at least two other decision makers within their company after the show. Ask for those names. Always allow space on a lead form for other contacts.

Likewise your prospect needs to know five things about you as well:

1. Your name and company name accompanied by a strong handshake.

2. Your business card or special card designed to giveaway at this show. Keep your business cards in one pocket and all the business cards or lead cards you write on in another pocket to make a smooth presentation of your business cards to people you meet.

3. The "elevator version," or 30-second description, of what your company offers so there is no misunderstanding on the prospect's part.

4. An understanding of what they are going to get from you next. Are you going to send literature, include them in the e-mail newsletter, and ask them to join you in the hospitality suite?

5. Your company Web site, noting two of the most interesting pages that the prospect will likely find interesting as well.

Hospitality Suites Ring Up Sales
Finally, it is social time

Visit all hospitality rooms and events possible to meet and exchange cards with trade show attendees. Often success is a result of "just being present." When I am participating in a trade show, I plan to go to as many functions as possible until I cannot go any longer because I may "bump into" my dream customer at the next event. Before participating in a trade show, I try to accumulate as much sleep as possible because experience has shown me as hard as I try, I will lose sleep during the show going to all available activities.

At a recent National Talk Show Hosts Conference, I was in my hotel room no more than 6 hours at a time catching up on sleep and freshening up for the next event. At every event during that hectic conference, I would meet a valuable contact with which

I wished to maintain contact. When I boarded the plane to come home, I immediately fell asleep and kept dozing off for the next two days, but oh was it worth it.

If you think of hospitality suites as free drinks and food after a long day working at a trade show, think again. More and more, today's hospitality suites are the place business gets done. The reason is simple: Executives say that by visiting a suite, they got to know the movers and shakers in the company, got to mingle with fellow customers and, as a result, developed more trust in the company. Even five years ago many executives felt visiting suites was less productive and included more social than business discussions. But five years ago they were not experiencing the inability to reach people. Modern communication tools such as voice mail; faxes and e-mail keep executives up to date, but do not allow them the all important face-to-face meetings so desirable in business. A hospitality suite encourages those meetings. Where else will a customer find your company's CEO and other top management in one room – and available for private conversation? In a recent survey group, 54 percent said they held a more favorable impression of the company after visiting a suite and left with more confidence in doing business with that firm.

Here are seven strategies for making your hospitality suite a successful trade show exhibit:

1. **Give them space.**
    Do not let the room get too crowded. Let guests mingle, do not let them bunch up in cluster groups. Do not corner guests.

2. **Create access.**
    Start a reception line so everyone gets a chance to shake hands with the CEO. Staff the suite with top management.

3. **Plan for comfort.**
    Offer plenty of seating. Break the ice with a welcoming speech full of comments about your company's new direction or product.

4. **Order ample food.**
    Go business class – not first class – with the food or drink. Guests complain too many companies run short of food. Purchase the mid-level hors d'oeuvres and have ample amounts.

5. Look comfortable.
Take the edge off the corporate sales look. Leave your vest or double-breasted suit at home; could be too intimidating. Opt, instead, for softly colored ties and shirts. Women should add a bit of sophisticated jewelry to the usual business attire. It literally adds sparkle to the atmosphere.

Do not just stand there with your arms crossed or your hands in your pockets. Always hold something in your hand; a business card case, notebook or company brochure will help to avoid slouching or folding your arms.

6. Be approachable. Carry a smile.
Guests want to feel accepted and part of the group. A smile lets them know you are approachable.

Work the entire suite; do not just corner a few people. Let others help you break the ice. Introduce a new guest to someone you know, and then let the guest tell both of you about his or her business. Do not use "What's new?" or "How's business?" as opening lines. Instead, ask a guest for his or her opinion of the trade show or new products.

7. Sell smart.
Listening is a big part of conducting business so tone down your sales pitch and hone your listening skills. Your goal is to let your guests reveal their plans and problems. They will not open up if they fear a sales pitch will mow them down.

Always be ready to jot down names or ideas. We all forget 50 percent of what we hear in one minute. Take notes and promise your guests you will look into their questions as soon as possible. They will be impressed that you take them seriously and feel important. That is exactly why they came to the suite in the first place: To get personal attention.

Is all this planning and activity worth the effort? Yes, definitely. I routinely arrive home with stacks of business cards from individuals nationwide with whom I had in-depth discussions. The notes about each person on their card or my lead form have proven invaluable for building long-term business relationships.

When You Arrive Home...

Send a nice note to each person you just met at the trade show. Include the most valuable of these contacts on your holiday greetings database. Notice, I said "note." Anybody can send company collateral in a 10" x 13" envelope ... you want to be professionally different.

Marketers recognize the term "cognitive dissonance." This phrase is a marketing term that describes that process a person goes through within the first three days after making a decision about a purchase they have just made or a person they have just met. The buyer's thinking goes something like this: "Did I do the right thing by purchasing this item or encouraging further activity by the person I just met?" I apply cognitive dissonance to two people meeting for the first time. Each of you asks yourself, "Do I want to continue a relationship with the person in front of me?" For most, this thought process does not take three days. Cognitive dissonance applies to the exhibitor (or the hospitality suite sponsor) and the show attendee because you have to reinforce the positive thought processes in the other person's mind about you by affirming they did make the right decision spending time with you at your exhibit or hospitality suite. Once you leave the trade show, you are "out of sight and out of mind" to those attendees you just met. This is not the time to let these investments in time and money slip away. Cultivate and harvest each contact as a long-term business relationship.

Periodically contact each person from the trade show you include on your database. In such a fast moving business world, you need to keep your name in front of your customers and prospects at least once every three months. My timetable is at least one exposure to each person on my database every three to six weeks.

I mail professional, personal-sized holiday notes to my most valuable contacts on my database with a First-class stamp adhered that matches the color of the envelope. Periodically, I follow-up these communiqués with a phone call to add another human touch. The key is to be professional, business like and human at the same time. Each successive year you see people on your contact list, you bring them one step closer to becoming long-term customers.

Following these ideas for maximizing your face-to-face trade show experiences, your contact database will grow rapidly and profitably. As your database begins to grow, your contacts will become referral sources that generate more contacts that generate more referrals. Cultivate and harvest your trade show contacts ... then look forward to the next year's exhibit to deepen relationships and acquire more contacts and business.

Virtual Trade Shows Open New Doors...

You pour a cup of hot coffee, turn on your computer and log onto the Internet to visit the site of this year's annual conference. You attend some breakout sessions, read transcripts from each speaker and watch video clips of the keynote addresses from the comfort of your home or office.

You then search the online directory of exhibitors to locate some companies with whom you are interested in doing business. You "visit" their online booths, watch product demonstrations, and download catalogs and price listings. Before leaving the exhibit hall, you check your company's booth for messages from other "attendees," return personalized e-mail messages to those people who have requested details on your company's products or services and set up appointments for follow-up telephone sales calls.

You then adjourn to a hospitality suite where many of your peers are chatting about industry news. You have conducted all of your day's conference business without taking valuable time away from the office, contending with airlines, car rental companies or hotel clerks, and handling logistical problems with exhibit hall drayage and costly amenities such as carpeting, plants, furniture rental and telephone lines.

This virtual scenario is becoming a reality as conference organizers begin to harness the powers of the Internet. Conferences, seminars and trade shows are no longer static events limited by the walls of a building or the hours of the day as conference organizers take events out of the convention hall and move them onto the Internet in the form of "virtual trade shows."

Some are complaining that site-based shows are ineffective sales venues. This $45 billion market represents all SIC codes for nearly every product and service sold in the world. Trade shows are typically the second largest expenditure in a corporation's marketing budget behind advertising. This year there will be more than 5,000 major trade shows, conferences and seminars held in the United States and Canada alone. The increasing number of these events is placing burdens on conference providers, exhibitors and attendees alike.

InterAct '96: A Glimpse Into The Present

InterAct '96 was billed as the first virtual trade show and conference to take place entirely on the Web without having a corresponding physical event. The three-day show, sponsored by InfoWorld, Stratus Computers Inc. and Time magazine, offered attendees the digital equivalent of the trade show experience. They sat in on presentations (accessible in both audio, video and text formats), networked with colleagues and posted messages to topical and networking chat rooms.

With the use of virtual avatars (3-D graphical representations of humans that people could communicate with online), attendees toured the interactive exhibit hall and sampled products and services showcased by 17 high-tech companies, including Netscape, Digital Equipment Corporation and Stratus Computers. Visitors could also follow hypertext links to exhibitors' individual Web sites.

The site also featured audio and video interview clips, press releases and kids' room with connections to family-oriented Web sites. While there were some reported technological glitches during the event, InterAct '96 gave us a glimpse of the Internet's promise as a significant venue for today's virtual trade shows.

Now more than 400 trade shows have some presence on the Web. The scope and sophistication of each site varies greatly, but virtual trade shows can be broken into two categories:

The Information-Based Site.

Some organizations use the Internet as an adjunct to their site-based event, offering attendees services such as online pre-registration, seminar handouts, exhibitor information and details on restaurants, hotels, dining, local attractions and entertainment. Other event organizers are using all of the available Internet technology to move their entire events online, complete with audio and video clips of keynote addresses, downloadable seminar handouts and live chat sessions. Attendees also can visit interactive exhibit halls where they can communicate with manufacturers, distributors and service providers, request information and place orders.

While it is a natural evolution for computer professionals to move events online, other industries are following suit. This includes both business-to-business and consumer groups, ranging from chemical engineers and fire-and-rescue personnel to dog trainers and quilters.

The Transaction-Based Site

The trade show market, which includes professional conference organizers and professional associations, are finding that virtual trade shows can be a valuable way of reaching a global audience of interested attendees that may be prohibited from attending the physical show. They can also create more interest and awareness and generate more traffic to their physical events. They can build new revenue models by selling virtual exhibits and sponsorships, event proceedings, course books and directories online. Some are even developing list brokerage businesses by tracking registered virtual attendees.

The Professional Convention Management Association (PCMA), for example, has saved money by launching a show-based site. "It is much easier putting up a Web site and dealing with people electronically than it is to put out a mailing," says Bill Myers, former CEO of PCMA. "We saved $20,000 by offering visitors the opportunity to download conference handouts instead of printing the information in a book, and we made information available to an entire universe of people." The site has received thousands of visitors to date and has generated numerous new memberships, an added bonus for an association of 5,000-plus members. "More importantly," says Myers, "it gives the association the opportunity to serve as a role model for our members and lead them into the use of new technology."

Medtrade Online (http://www.medtrade.com) showcases one of the largest trade shows for health care products. This "show" is open to visitors 24 hours each day, 365 days each year. Visitors can search exhibitor resources, request information and purchase products online. All of the 1,200 exhibiting companies receive a listing in an alphabetical directory, and many of them have chosen to have special links to the site. Companies pay over $1,500 annually for the virtual exhibits, which include text, logos, a directory of contacts and product order forms. This costs less than an onsite rental, which ran $23 per square foot, or $2,300 for a 10x10 foot booth for the four-day event.

The advantage of a transaction-based site is that you get an immediate return for your investment, says Tom Mitchell, managing partner of VOLTS, which launched Medtrade Online. "You immediately know who visited the site and who asked for information or bought your products."

The benefits of exhibiting at a virtual trade show can go well beyond building brand awareness. By keeping exhibit halls open 365 days a year, marketers are able to continually communicate with conference attendees and site visitors, generate leads and make sales. They can run special show promotions, announce new products and services, and offer virtual demonstrations. They can also advertise in "real time" by updating products, services, prices and offers, which are typically static in traditional media.

Deloitte & Touche Consulting Group's Chemical Process Industries Group signed on to exhibit at the ChemExpo site (http://www.chemexpo.com) because they consider the Internet a viable marketing tool, says Larry Mickelberg, marketing and operations coordinator. "We are also trying to create dialogue with visitors and use the exhibit as a relationship building tool. We also want to engage people in a non-threatening way and then get prospects to proceed through the sales cycle."

Novell Inc. has used the Interop Online (http://www.interop.com) site in conjunction with the Networld+Interop conference booth as part of an integrated marketing program. Novell used the site-based show and accompanying press events to launch Internet Ware, an Internet software product. They also sponsored the online show and conference planner, which allowed attendees to access up-to-date information about the conference, tutorials, workshops, exhibitors and the interactive show floor. The planner, which runs on the Internet Ware software, also enables attendees to design a personalized itinerary, which can be saved on the Web site, and can be reviewed and changed during subsequent visits. "We thought that extending our presence online would be a good opportunity to extend our promotional reach to attendees and non-attendees alike, demonstrate our product and generate leads," says William Donahoo, senior director of product marketing for Novell.

Creating Virtual Trade Show Communities

The cost of exhibiting at Interop Online might seem high compared to other online events, but Key3Media Events is doing more than staging site-based conferences and virtual trade shows. It is creating Internet communities around each of its events and forums, some of which have included Microsoft Site Builder Conference, Interactive '98, Seybold Seminars, WebINNOVATION and JavaOne. There is also a database of networking products that includes a listing of all of the exhibitors at each show.

Key3 is even building a special community of loyal visitors. The 3,000-plus people who have taken time to offer demographic information (name, address, title, company, e-mail address and purchase authority) receive special registration lines at the conference, contests and other perks. The show producer turns to these loyal Club Interop members to conduct focus groups, round table discussions and for other information-gathering initiatives. Donahoo points out that virtual trade show advertisers and sponsors reap incremental benefits from show sponsor promotions and the great number of people they attract. Other exhibitors promoting the site also means increased traffic for Novell and the other Interop Online advertisers. "It would be very difficult to drive that many people to a company's independent Web site," he says.

Exhibitors benefit from more than high traffic volume at Interop Online. While many people gauge Internet marketing success by the number of hits they receive, Key3 takes great pains to measure specific Web traffic. Using the Nielsen Media Research I/Pro System, which is much like a circulation audit, they are able to capture detailed information regarding when people visited, where they went within the site, what information they requested, etc. This information is used for Key3's internal marketing and also is shared with advertisers and sponsors.

The Future of Virtual Trade Shows

The number of virtual trade shows continues to increase each year, as they generated more than $100 million in annual revenues in 1999, according to Virtual Broadcast Company. Few prognosticators predict they will completely replace site-based events. "People are very interactive and social in nature," says Bill Myers, former CEO, Professional Convention Management Association. "You'll never obviate the need for businesspeople to get together face-to-face and conduct commerce."

The most successful virtual trade shows today are those that work as enhancements to site-based events. They offer conference providers and exhibiting companies the opportunity to expand awareness of their products and services to a global marketplace 24 hours a day, 365 days a year. They give attendees and visitors immediate access to information to get their jobs done.

Helpful Hints

- **Plan** – Prepare far ahead to communicate with prospects and customers. Send prospects and customers you want to see at the exhibit a small, personalized letter inviting them to meet with you at the show.

- **Put the Literature in the Vault** – Company literature should not be distributed except to your serious business prospects.

- **Match Your Exhibit Personnel** – Consider your target audience profile and who the attendees at the trade show will be to match your personnel with this profile.

- **Acquire Basic Information** – For every exhibit visitor, acquire the person's business card or the information on your prepared lead form. Information you acquire from prospects is equal to the gold at Fort Knox.

- **After Hours, Relax** – Hospitality suites are great if you maintain poise and concentrate on building relationships with profitable prospects.

- **The Aftermath** – When you return home, include your recent acquaintances on your contact software and immediately follow up with a personalized note and phone call.

- **Virtual Trade Shows** – With detailed planning, you can reach prospects and customers without leaving your business location. This form of company information delivery is increasing rapidly.

Chapter 8

Want More Business? ... Network

Meeting For Business

Networking has been around since the beginning of time as people sought to get ahead by forming strategic alliances with people in more powerful positions.

Although in functionality it is much the same now, today's networking represents a portrait of the changing American business landscape. It has become an essential part of the marketing mix for the burgeoning number of people in business development and self-employed free agents. These groups often operate with a small staff and budgets and must reach out beyond their own enterprises to get advice, information, support and referrals to help their business prosper.

Whether an event is business or social, networking gurus agree it is more than standing around a room full of people holding a drink in your hand. You are dealing with a selective audience and it is the wise networkers who utilize guidelines like the following eight to make the most of the occasion.

1. **Develop several different conversation starters.**
   Ahead of time, think how you can comment on the event itself, ask others why they decided to attend it and query people about themselves and their business.

2. **Be unafraid about approaching people.**
   The world is full of strangers but if you talk to them, they can become your customers. If you are self-conscious, focus instead on the other person's comfort level.

3. **Keep track of your new connections.**
It is a good idea to bring a small notebook and pen to jot down more extensive notes than can fit on the back of someone's business card.

4. **Spend no more than 10 minutes with each person.**
Veteran networkers know they are at an event to circulate and meet a variety of people – not engage in a prolonged conversation with just one person.

5. **Exchange business cards only when appropriate.**
There is a misconception that in order to network properly, you must deal a card to every extended hand. Not so. Only ask for someone's card, in exchange for yours, if you really want to stay in touch and you believe that person is a good resource.

6. **Listen more than you talk.**
The old adage about using your two ears and one mouth in that proportion is especially true in a networking setting. People are flattered when you listen carefully.

7. **Give effective leads.**
If you listen actively, you will hear a need and likely be able to make an appropriate match with someone you know. In addition, if you work an event by asking others how you can help them succeed, you will be a standout. Be aware, too, of giving "bad" leads because your actions have a tendency to make "full circle."

8. **Know how to end a conversation.**
According to etiquette expert, "Miss Manners," it's perfectly okay to say, "Excuse me, it's been nice meeting you," or "I've enjoyed speaking with you," and move to another part of the room.

Experts encourage businesspeople to be open to serendipity and to be patient. Networking usually does not produce immediate results since it is based on building relationships and trust over time. Patience and persistence usually results in ample payoff for your efforts. When you feel as though you have met and mingled with everybody that could possibly provide you business, what do you do? Host an after hours mixer for your customers and prospects.

Earlier this year, I wanted to test the idea of "good things flow when people are relaxed" theory. This being the first business social I had single-handedly planned in years, I had no idea what would ultimately happen. Choosing a neutral location, such as a professional downtown restaurant club, seemed to be the best choice.

Opening the Yellow Pages as well as browsing through the local event papers, I called five nice clubs that appeared the most promising for a professional, relaxed event. When I called the first club, I listened intently for hints or ideas the person could offer to make my event a success. From this first call, I prepared answers for the club employees' most frequently asked questions. Questions from each of the five clubs called went something like this:

- "How many are in your party?" (I guessed between 20 to 40; had no idea).

- "Will you be providing food and drinks?" (First drink, yes; each club had a "happy hour").

- "What time do you plan to begin and wrap-up?" (5:00 p.m. to 7:30 p.m.).

After mulling over the pluses and minuses of each of the five locations for a couple of days, I chose a landmark establishment that everyone in my city knows. I chose Thursday for the event because most guests would be in town that day and more inclined to be in a good mood (the following day is Friday). Recognizing that I have the entrepreneurial spirit and am willing to take calculated risks, hosting a social for relaxing business seems easy enough. Truth is, hosting a business social in my hometown scared me more than any business decision to date. This is only the beginning. On top of the routine logistics of inviting guests and making arrangements, the fact that this is my FIRST business social in years loomed ever near. Questions arose, such as:

- How do I deliver invitations to enough customers and prospects so at least 20 professionals attend?

- How do I make this event a relaxing success for everybody so we can have an encore event?

- Why would anyone want to come to my event in the first place ... what is my unique selling proposition?

- What do I do if only five or so professionals show?

Now you can relax. My first business mixer turned out to be a big success! Here are some of the details.

Distributing invitations became a fun event and good reason to contact customers and prospects. Even if no one had shown up that fateful Thursday night, I still made progress with all the calls, faxes and e-mails to people with whom I wanted to communicate. On top of that, every person I spoke with liked the idea of meeting other professionals after hours for great food and free drinks. After the fifteenth call, my confidence began to improve. I have a winner with this idea! Over 400 invitations were delivered by a variety of means. Now it was too late to change my mind.

The next question involved what to do when people arrived? I have been to business mixers where elaborate events were planned and others where no events were planned. The answer in my case was easy. After paying for the guests' first drink on a peanut butter budget, there was no budget for entertainment left. How can I communicate this to guests in a positive way? Here is the theme I decided upon for the event:

"No Reason to Get Together But Enjoyment"

The guests did not know that I was referring to my budget in the theme. The guests liked the simplicity. From the theme came my unique selling proposition:

"Come together for no reason but to enjoy yourself
and you may meet someone to do business with."

Now the magical moment arrives: Thursday at 5:00 p.m. The host at the club is very nice and promises to warmly greet each of my guests as they arrive. Soon after I sit in the section designated for my group, several nice looking people I do not know sit in "my area". When approached, I discover these people are with **another** group similar to mine, competing for the **same floor space**. Damage control to the rescue. A friend and I quickly arrange tables and chairs for 30 people and protect this space with our lives. I am determined by this time that this event will be a success, regardless of the numbers.

Gradually, my customers, prospects and some others whom I have no idea where they came from, begin to arrive. The atmosphere in the room is upbeat. A pianist is playing relaxing music and the guests are beginning to "gel."

With the help of the club's wait staff and host, I am free to mingle and enjoy myself with guests. To my delight, guests are laughing, exchanging business cards, and talking about high-speed Internet connections and everything else under the sun. When the evening was over, there had been 35 guests who ALL seemed to enjoy themselves. Over the next week, I heard from most of the guests telling me how much fun and business they actually realized from participating in my mixer.

Conclusion. I am planning "No Reason to Get Together But Enjoyment" mixers in the future. Now, the "butterflies" I had before the event have flown away and I can enjoy my mixers as easily as my guests.

Planning Your Company's "Special Event"

Now, if you really want more business en masse, try a "networking event" on a larger scale. "Special events, done correctly, are a very valuable tool because they can put groups of people together in a situation where they're talking about business," says John Allen, owner of Rand Incentive Marketing and a former Kodak marketing and sales executive. "You're putting people in a situation where they can hear from others just how good you are. That is ten times the value of what you get from any communications you generate."

Special events also offer unique opportunities to get a message across. You have a captive audience that is at least somewhat interested in your company so they will likely sit through more than just a quick event. It can give your prospects a chance to meet top executives or view how your high-tech product is made. It also gives you a chance to showcase your company's creativity, teamwork and business planning skills by pulling off a memorable event. Here are eight points to keep in mind when planning your next event:

1. **Have a theme for the event.**
What is the reason for the event? Nothing frustrates an executive more than to clear a day or more from an already hectic schedule only to find the time wasted. If you have doubts whether your event can stand alone, but would still like to draw top prospects, try adding more enticement to the event such as a party at a major sporting event.

2. **Check the dates.**
You will never find a time convenient for everyone, but your business undoubtedly has good and bad seasons. Events surrounding trade shows are sound because you know many of your customers will be there, you have a lot of your staff there, and there is inherent excitement surrounding the new products you are exhibiting. People are so busy at trade shows, though, you may not get their full attention. If you encounter too much competition with other, well-established trade show events, consider another date.

3. **Decide who will attend.**
If the event is at a trade show, are spouses invited? How many – and which – key players from each customer's company should come? You may get more bangs for your dollar if you say "thank you" to that oft-forgotten MIS manager or other unsung hero on the customer's decision-making team.

4. **Contact early and often.**
Time is money. People's schedules are planned down to the minute. "If you're planning a trade show event, it is likely your prized customers and prospects will be invited to several parties so make sure you provide them with plenty of time to plan ahead," notes Michael Estwanik, business development manager for McGettigan Partners, a promotion agency. Send invitations six weeks in advance. Provide phone follow-up to remind people to RSVP so they will not be left out. A reminder call or fax just prior to the event can help gain a firm commitment.

5. **Scout the location.**
This is the stage for your event. It will determine the atmosphere as well as how much information is exchanged. Here are a few guidelines.

The home office is good if you are trying to showcase your technology or want people to meet lots of executives, but it is often too distracting for both employees and visitors. There is a big chance people will wander off to visit friends or leave to make phone calls. If you choose this option, plan to tightly control the group's whereabouts.

Nice hotels and conference centers work well. They are used to hosting parties and can often suggest fun decorations or food to carry a theme. If people are traveling to get to the event, provide them with the chance to experience the local culture. In the southwest, plan a western barbecue. Hold a clambake or fish fry on the coasts.

Look for the unique if it fits your mission, notes Estwanik. He suggests holding an event at a venue that either sells itself or is so unusual that the customers' curiosity is piqued. For one party, Varilux, a maker of ophthalmic lenses, took over Studio 450, one of New York's premier fashion photography studios. For another, the company chose the historic New York landmark, The Metropolitan Club, highlighted by famed travel photographer Peter Guttman, "The locations helped sell the party and create the perfect backdrop for highlighting the lens product," Estwanik says.

6. **Staff carefully.**
    "You have to be careful of overstaffing the event because you want your customers to feel they can talk to each other without one of your staff jumping in," says Allen. "It's okay for customers to talk to each other – you have to have confidence in your business."

    Estwanik also suggests creating a supporting cast. "Waiters and entertainers can do far more than serve and entertain," he says. "In frequent contact with guests, they can often make or break a positive impression. When they are excited, they raise the energy of the party. Left out, they can distract or undermine your efforts. Take the time to explain the purpose of the event – the thinking behind the theme, who the guests are and why they are coming to all onsite support staff (waiters, bartenders, parking attendants, florists, security guards). You will be surprised how much value they can bring to your overall sales strategy and image messages."

7. Watch the agenda.
This is a tricky detail. You want to keep people busy enough
that they are not bored or tempted to leave early, but you do
not want them so busy they cannot talk to each other. Be sure
to provide natural gatherings so the more inhibited are
comfortable introducing themselves. One strong suggestion is
to plan multiple events within the event. A home office tour, a
mini-trade show of your company's new products and a
roundtable chat with executives allow people to get the same
information in different ways while also providing some less
structured time.

If you are planning a party, consider entertainment that
rotates around the floor or occurs several times throughout the
evening. A band can perform three sets of music, for example,
while a magician can draw several different crowds in one
evening.

There is also the time to get creative. Try to incorporate
events that reinforce your message in a subtle way:

Is your product sturdier than the competitor's?
How about a game of tug o'war?

Does your product incorporate space-age technology?
How about a visit from a real astronaut?

**Are you celebrating new relationships with international
customers?**
How about a geographic trivia contest where your customers ask
the questions about their home countries and your top executives
try not to embarrass themselves?

Remember to help people get to and from the location. In
New York, this may mean running buses or limos from the major
hotels. If you are flying people between locations, it will mean
designating people to meet guests at the airport.

8. Give gifts they will remember.
"Parting gifts are great ways to help guests remember their
positive experience," says Estwanik. "They can also be used
as strategic tools to reinforce or complement a sales or image
message." At an event that coincided with the launch of
Varilux's, "It's The Lens" advertising campaign (featuring a
close-up photograph of actor Tom Berenger wearing the

company's *Comfort* brand lenses), advertising photographer Stand Schnier was brought in to photograph each guest in the same position and lighting as Berenger. When they left, each guest was given a souvenir folder with the "It's The Lens" logo on the cover and their photo inside, including the "It's The Party" logo, date and location. The gift not only reminded them of the good time they had, but also kept the advertising theme top of mind long after the party lights were turned out.

Allen suggests sending parting gifts after the people get home. "Usually people pack up and leave, then the next contact is the salesperson. If you send a nice "thank you" letter with a memento, it will be remembered for a long time. "For example, he sent a Waterford Crystal paperweight shaped like a football to customers who attended a Super Bowl party he threw. He also sent a wooden box containing a compass after an outdoor event.

If you try just 25 percent of the ideas presented here for networking, will you let me study your Rolodex?

Helpful Hints

- **Do not be shy** – With business cards in hand, be proactive and develop social graces to build your business.

- **Host a "mixer"** – Plan your own mixer ... invite your "A" and "B" list ... enjoy a relaxing social setting.

- **Plan your company "special event"** – Watch productivity and retention improve with your company when employees, customers and prospects get together outside the office for well-planned socials.

Chapter 9

Who Said Business Cannot Be Fun?

Are you looking for a professional and unique way to invigorate your business? Want your customers and prospects to tell others how much fun you are to be around? I have actually instigated the following activities (and others) to bond with customers and prospects of mine, living to tell these stories to you.

Sports Events

For openers, try a sports event that is slightly different for your locale. In Texas, a good example is ice hockey. I took several customers to an ice hockey game in Austin, Texas. None of the participants had seen an ice hockey game and did not know the first thing about the sport (right from the start, I am feeling comfortable with this scenario). I did not know the game of ice hockey either.

We arrive at the game early on Friday night, eat a relaxing meal in the onsite restaurant and find our seats. Every seat in the auditorium is a good seat and thankfully our seats are among the best (a friend had coached me which seats to select in advance).

I had forgotten that ice hockey is an inside sport that is not only cold to the players, but to the audience as well. Luckily, everyone in my group had dressed for the outside weather, which was quite cold. If you go to an ice hockey game for the first time as a host, remember to dress warm, so as to not appear nervous because your teeth are chattering from the temperature.

After the newness of our environment began to wear off, the guests and I began to genuinely enjoy watching a game for which we had no knowledge. Icing on the cake was that "our team" won.

If you are entertaining in California, go ice-skating. If you are entertaining in Minnesota, go to an outdoor volleyball game. Do something just a little different, while staying with a mainstream sport and your business relationships can gel.

Reading Food Labels

On another occasion, I had this feeling that one of my largest customers would like an activity that is admittedly, different. Late one weekday afternoon, I picked my customer up at his office. The two of us then went directly to a major grocery store that was modern and very clean. Our mission that afternoon: To read, and make light of, labels on food products. What started out as a spoof turned out to be a real eye opener. Both of us went from row to row together reading food labels at random, not understanding most of the words we were reading, all the while having a wonderful time. By the way, as a result of our unscientific research, I no longer eat Oreo® cookies with white filling and several brands of ice cream.

Since the grocery store visit, this same customer and I have participated in several other offbeat and fun diversions. This particular customer is approached by my competitors constantly and is still **my** customer. You cannot knock offbeat ideas that are legal and work while being fun.

Bringing Home the Bread

Another idea for business entertainment "outside the box" is to treat a customer or prospect to lunch at a nice restaurant that has an attached bakery. After you and your customer(s) have finished your meal, treat the office staff of your guest(s) to some fresh bread or cookies from the adjoining bakery. Whenever I implement this idea, my guest(s) suggest the "goodies" may not make it back to the office. I can understand because the aroma of freshly baked goods in your car going back to the office is hard to resist. So far, there is no need to fear. I often hear from the office staff the next time I visit their office how everyone appreciates my consideration with the baked goods.

Drinking at the Office

Want to improve morale and productivity in any office? Research what colas and juices individuals in a particular office like to drink. On specific days, such as Tuesdays or Fridays, bring a styrofoam ice chest full of these items for the office staff and the implementation of the snack idea will have immediate payback.

Almost every Friday for two years, I provided favorite colas in a styrofoam ice chest for the answering service office staff with whom I contracted. Customers of mine were constantly making comments about the pleasant staff I had on the phone. You can rightfully state that this service level should be assumed in an office staff job description. Intangible touches, however, cannot help but improve morale and your bottom line.

Snacks in the Lobby

One of my favorite means of gauging what people are saying about my products and services is to come right out and visit the other person's business. Just before lunchtime, I visit one of my customers' businesses with an ice chest of "goodies" for everyone in the office. The all-time favorite foods include snack foods that are low calorie and chocolate chip cookies. A variety of diet and regular colas, along with bottled water, satisfy people's thirst. When scheduling a day that I plan to be in the customer's lobby at 11:30 a.m., I call to confirm that the decision makers and influential staff members will be in the office that morning.

I want to emphasize that a common sense business etiquette approach is to respect other people and their work schedules. With snacks you provide, located in the lobby near the receptionist, different members of the customers' company can "talk and go" (including decision makers). Casually ask different members of the staff and decision makers what they like and do not like about your products and services as they pick up food and acknowledge your presence.

I make my position very clear, in a polite way, with people as they come and go in the lobby. After visiting two of my best customers in this manner, I select two customers that have recently tapered off the orders and duplicate the same thing before lunch.

When everyone relaxes with snacks, you will be amazed what you hear. Often, partakers in the lobby will sense that I *really do* want the truth, be it good or bad, and provide their unaltered opinions. On top of it all, people walking through the lobby when I am there with "goodies" seem to treat me differently later ... as to acknowledge that I really care about our business relationship. You can call this a *real power lunch!*

What do you do about customers located in another city? Simply overnight non-perishables to arrive by 10:30 a.m. with an enclosed explanation. Inside the "goody box," my note of explanation thanks them for their business (or return to business soon, hopefully) and I express a genuine desire that everyone in the office will enjoy the snacks.

For businesspeople in another city, I soon call the primary decision maker to thank them for their business and ask permission to ask several brief questions. Questions are always specific and revolve around what the decision maker likes and dislikes about my business.

Cannot Kid the Kids

Are you sitting down for my next business development project? I can personally verify the axiom, "Kids say the darndest and most honest things." Earlier this year, I organized a "theme trip" on Saturday for kids from nine to twelve years old to a favorite area fast food restaurant (do this first on the schedule) and my office lobby afterward (including the parents). About 2 o'clock, we went to a small theme park. The Saturday event was not only fun, it was rewarding for personal and business reasons. Remember to discourage the kids from overeating, or you will have to postpone the entire afternoon activities. I can hear you now. You are asking, "How can kids contribute to my company success?" Read on.

My theme trip program has its beginnings from one of professional copywriters' best research tools. A professional copywriter knows that a twelve-year-old has to understand what is being said about a company in print (the copywriter's assignment) or it is time to go back to the drafting table. I apply the same idea of "kid response" to my written products. Kids need to be able to understand what my company does for others and the basics of why I show up for work ... giving me valuable open feedback. Boy, what feedback I hear!

One nine-year-old suggested that I write shorter sentences with more down-to-earth language to quickly communicate with customers what I wanted them to do (excellent observation and implemented). Another ten-year-old said she likes to see "one-topic booklets" of information, instead of mixing three topics in a large ring binder (implemented on the next printing). As an added bonus, parents gave me valuable tips that are being implemented wherever possible.

You are probably asking yourself, "What did all this research cost?" For each company event where snacks were provided before lunchtime, my total budget was $75. For each participant in the "kid theme trip" (there were 14 kids and parents), my budget was $30 apiece.

Now, you are probably wondering if I believe my results were worth the effort? Undoubtedly, yes! The next time you want to know what people are really thinking about your company and your products, I can confirm that food, kids with their parents and market research mix very well.

My activities entail a great deal of thought about each individual I invite to participate with me. So far, I have not made any mistakes about matching an activity to an individual's personality. All I have noticed is the tightening of a tangible business relationship with those who are dear to my business.

Donating Your Time Can Pay Off

From time to time, businesspeople are asked if they would be willing to donate their time and expertise to help make a nonprofit organization a success. How should you respond? Should you volunteer your skills?

In a nutshell, doing charitable work is an excellent way to make new, very high-level contacts. It also gives you a unique opportunity to engage in quality networking while doing something personally rewarding.

Helping Yourself

Businesspeople receive many benefits when they plan a fundraising event for a favorite organization.

- Bosses and prospective customers love seeing community work on a resume.
- Working with the business, industry and government leaders who serve on the boards and committees of volunteer organizations can lead to new projects and new jobs. The higher the profile of the charity group, the more influential its board members are. Just take a look at the roster of any typical nonprofit organization, and notice the prominent individuals who are helping to run it. Each is a potential customer or future employer.
- Arranging a local fundraiser gives businesspeople the opportunity to meet and impress those who attend the event. If it is a gala evening or a golf tournament, the guest list should be full of the decision makers and senior managers of the area's leading companies. This way, businesspeople showcase their talents and skills to another set of potential employers and customers.
- The event itself can generate free publicity for you and your company. Be sure your name and/or company name is prominently mentioned in all the literature. At the event, make yourself available, and circulate. Have your business card ready to pass out to potential customers and employers. Do not forget to follow up with these new contacts.
- Do not underestimate the health benefits of doing a good deed. Beyond the great feeling a job well done affords, when you do that job for a group whose message you believe in, the satisfaction multiplies.

Aftermath

One result of all this blood, sweat and tears is that you probably will be asked to work on future events for the organization. Say, "yes", because the additional exposure can only help. Another point to remember: Just because the first time was free does not mean that future efforts have to be.

I can attest to the fact that doing charitable work can help a career or business. For a number of years, I was a volunteer for my local Small Business Administration office. Some of the other volunteers were senior-level executives from local corporations. When I later became a trainer and speaker, these contacts were worth their weight in gold.

They were more willing to put me in touch with the key decision makers in their corporations. They also knew a number of high-level people in other companies and were happy and eager to pass my name along to them. Without these contacts, it would have been difficult to gain entrée to many of these organizations.

Everybody Needs A Favorite Getaway

Everyone who works with Kristi knows she leaves the office early. She packs in a full day with prospects and customers, regularly turning in great results. Bob, the office early bird, sees Kristi come to the office before many of her coworkers with a full load of paperwork under one arm *every* weekday morning. Kristi never tells her colleagues where she is going when she leaves around 4:15 p.m. three afternoons a week. This is Kristi's secret weapon in maintaining her sales momentum.

Now I am going to let you in on Kristi's secret. This hard-working, conscientious businessperson goes to the same restaurant at 4:30 p.m. three weekday afternoons per week to enjoy her favorite raspberry ice tea. "Wait a minute," you say. "This secret sounds like an employee goofing off."

What you do not know is that stack of paperwork that Kristi allows to build on her desk during the day is completed during a "cool down" period away from the office. In addition, prospects and customers who do not want to come to Kristi's office can stop by and relax with her at a nice restaurant.

Take one of Kristi's customers as an example. George, who works for a large utility company in the city, is ready to explode by 4:00 p.m. every weekday. As Vice President of Operations, George is under a great deal of pressure to juggle many diverse tasks daily. He looks forward to his visits with a professional vendor out of his company's campus in a relaxing environment. George knows that almost every Tuesday, Wednesday or Thursday, he can go to the same restaurant and relax with Kristi while discussing their vendor relationship. Kristi also knows she can bring George (and numerous others coming by the restaurant) updates on their accounts, information about new products ... you name it ... to this relaxing environment. If no one comes on a particular afternoon, Kristi can relax and finish paperwork for the next day. Everyone wins.

Maintaining a routine and communicating the place and time with customers, gives Kristi an aura of dependability and sociability. I remember the first time a vendor told me he frequented the same restaurant twice a week and extended an open invitation to join him. During our conversation, I jotted the information on my calendar, planning to relax with him on one of "his" afternoons. Several weeks later, I looked at my note from our conversation and thought,

> "I'll leave for home early Wednesday and see if I can ask my vendor some questions at the restaurant he invited me to earlier."

What a surprise when I walked in and saw Steve (the vendor) at a booth with a bottomless glass of ice tea. Steve saw me walk in and motioned for me to join him. As it turns out, he had some new product information sheets to give me and suggestions for improvements to my Web site. Three glasses of ice tea and an hour and a half later, we were still chatting and scribbling notes on napkins. Talk about "business bonding." The next day, I implemented several of his suggestions for my Web site with a sense of gratitude because his suggestions were an oversight on my part. About every two months, we meet at the same restaurant and catch up on new developments.

Now you are likely asking yourself, "Isn't this expensive for Kristi and Steve to stop by a nice restaurant two to three times a week and run a 'tea tab' at their booth?" Consider my case. For Steve to physically come to my office involves driving an extra 16 miles round trip in his car during business hours. Assuming that we visit for no longer than twenty minutes (maximum time I allow all but the most important appointments) at my office, he has not accomplished anything unusual to "bond" or "connect" with me as a person.

Let us compare two business meeting scenarios in brief detail:

Meet at upscale, relaxing restaurant	Salesperson comes to my office
$ 1.50 for each tea +1.00 for gratuity (+ for multiple guests) $ 2.50 total each participant	16 miles on car @ $0.33/mile = $5.28
Time of our meeting is open-ended. Steve can work on other paperwork if no one shows.	Pre-set meeting time = 20 minutes max. Steve dedicates 100% time to me.
If multiple customers show, introduce customers to each other and keep conversation light ... great networking.	Networking opportunities are slim.

The proof comes on the commission statement. Every year after year of "relaxation", Kristi and Steve are the top sales performers in their district for their companies. Maintaining a disciplined routine of drinking ice tea (alcohol is strictly discouraged here) with customers is a proven winner.

Helpful Hints

- **Take a chance with key accounts** – In order to separate yourself from other vendors, take a calculated chance in sharing interesting activities with key account personnel.

- **Study personnel with whom you wish to build relations** – Often discovering personal interests in your key account personnel will clue you into fun activities to share together away from the office.

- **Kids provide great market research** – You cannot fool kids, so ask them for candid, unbiased views of your products and services.

- **Build key relationships at charitable events** – Non-threatening meetings at charitable events give everyone involved a chance to get to know each other in a neutral setting.

- **Consistent, relaxing tea breaks** – Establish a pattern at a nice restaurant and improve your bonds with key vendors and customers.

Chapter 10

Asking the Right People the Right Questions

Sometimes the best way to reach high-level decision makers and business owners is to conduct a marketing survey. You will get lots of information and a potential new customer or two.

By conducting a survey, you have an opportunity to meet individually with decision makers in your geographic area and ask each of them a series of questions to learn more about the needs of your market. This is an honest attempt on your part to better understand your prospects' needs so you can better satisfy those needs – the types of people who buy your products, what features they find most valuable, how they feel about the competition, and other factors which influence their purchase decisions. As a result of those interviews, some of the people you speak with will get to know you better and give you the opportunity to present your solutions to them.

Successful people – the kinds of people with the capacity to make major purchase decisions – are usually better informed than the average individual, and they tend to have egos to match. Ask a successful person their opinion on almost any subject and you are likely to get a response. Thus, the same people who refuse to give you a minute of their time to hear your business presentation are usually more inclined to talk with you when your stated purpose is to ask their opinion. Making a market survey work for you takes planning. The following are seven steps towards making this excellent business development method work for you.

1. Pick Your Survey Audience.

Your first task is to select people you want to participate in your survey. For every type of product and service, there are companies or people who are a natural audience. They are the leaders of their industry, spokespeople of their communities, trendsetters and people in the news. These people are important to your business success and they may be prospects. They may be able to refer prospects to you. Or they may just tell everyone they know about you, leading to the best of all business situations – when the prospects call you.

Finding these community leaders is usually easy. Their names are in the local newspapers all the time. They are in lists published by local agencies, like newspapers or chambers of commerce membership lists – the top 25 financial institutions in your county or the 50 most profitable companies in the metropolitan area. If your business scope is national, association lists are helpful. You probably have lists like this on your desk already. If you are like me, you have already filed this information for future reference. "Someday when I have time, I'm going to call these people," I say to myself. Go through your list and pick a dozen with whom you would like to talk. These are participants for your survey.

2. Pick Your Survey Theme.

Now that you know whom you will survey, you next have to figure out what you are surveying them about. Pick a narrow subject. Surveys work best when they are focused around a single issue or topic. You can ask several related questions, but you do not want to cover too many areas.

For example, if you represent a book publisher, you may want to survey prospects about textbooks and their usage. If you think about every grade level and every subject, there are a lot of different possibilities for a survey – books used in elementary schools, books for science, non-book resources they might use in the school library such as videos, and so on. Think narrowly about the topic. You will find it will lead to a more manageable survey, and one that will create better conversations with participants.

3. Tie Your Topic to a Current Issue.

When a topic is hot and in the news, everybody is ready to talk about it. What happens when a space shuttle takes off, or there is a sudden rise in the stock market, or the 6th game of the World Series is scheduled for Saturday night? Everybody has an opinion about topics in the news. The question is how to use this to get decision makers talking to you.

Think about what you just selected as the focus of your survey. Now review current news events and trends. Pick some event or trend of interest to your targets that you can tie your survey to. A topic that is in the news that may affect the people you are interviewing is always a good starting point. For example:

- You might want to talk to hospital administrators about using your outsourcing service, and you know the local government just reduced its budget for supporting local schools and hospitals. You ask the administrators how they plan to respond to the proposed budget changes.

- Your prospects are real estate agents who can recommend your construction company to buyers who want to upgrade their new home. You read that the local banks are tightening up on the available funds for mortgages, a subject of definite interest to real estate agents. You ask the people you interview their views on how the changes in mortgage lending will affect their businesses.

- Owners of small consulting practices tend to rent their office facilities from property management companies like yours. You read a front-page article about the decline of new class "A" office buildings under construction. You ask the owners to describe what the impact of this decline in construction will have on their renewals and what a property management company can do to help.

4. Write Your Survey Questions.

You are now ready to sit down and write the questions for the survey. With all your prep work, this should be quite straightforward. Here are some guidelines for writing survey questions:

* Start with a question about the current topic in the news. This is a good icebreaker and one that will get the conversation to start flowing.

* Keep it short. Your total list of questions should be no more than five to six. Virtually any decision maker, even the busiest of people, can participate in a short survey. It is also long enough for you to know if you are building any personal rapport or not.

* Write all questions in an open-ended format. For example, if you want to find out what type of furniture a store might be stocking to respond to changing trends in the market, ask questions like:

> "What types of tables are the people who come into your store looking for?"

> "What fabrics are requested most by shoppers?"

* Make sure you ask questions, which include specifics to your product, but are not just tied to that area. For example, if you are marketing copiers, you might survey the types of printed communications the company uses, saving one question for "what types of features make a copier a better fit for your company's communications needs?"

5. Prepare Your Story.

One final piece of preparation and you are ready to start your interviews. You need to have your own story together – who you are and why you are calling.

Let us say you work for a travel agency. You might start your story like this:

> "Good morning. My name is Michael McCann. I work for Zulu Travel Agency. I am conducting a survey of local executives in leading companies to learn more about what you look for in a business travel agency. Our goal is to make sure that the

services we, at Zulu Travel, offer to local businesses reflect their true needs. Then, as a result of this survey, we will put together a series of new travel services specifically for business travelers. I have just 6 questions I would like to ask you, so this will only take about 5 minutes."

The idea here is to state your purpose in terms that appear non-threatening and interesting to your prospect. Remember your stated goal in surveying is to gather information, not to sell. A final note on this point: Write this story down, even if it is one you have given many times or you think is self evident. It helps you get ready for talking to your audience.

6. Implement Your Plan.

Finally it is time to start talking to the people you selected to survey.

- Go through your list of decision makers and pick the ones who are your least likely prospects. Contact one or two of these first to get practice and gather some information you can use in your following surveys.

- Keep thorough notes on each of your conversations. Your survey will give you some important information that can impact all of your business activities, information most of your competitors will not have. You will hear ideas that will never come up in a more traditional business situation because your prospects are likely to be more honest.

- Use information you gather to help you in subsequent conversations. As you get quotes and comments from your audience, you will find some that will be quite interesting. You can use these in the rest of your survey calls. For example, "Mr. Jones, some of the executives I have spoken with today mentioned that the completeness and accuracy of their travel itinerary was an important thing they would like to see improved. Have itineraries been a problem for your company as well?"

During your interview, the person you are speaking with may raise issues for which you have solutions. Make a note of these. After you have completed your survey questions, return to one of these points: "Ms. Randall, one of the things you mentioned earlier was the importance of obtaining the lowest rental car rates in each city, as long as the car could be picked up conveniently close to the airport terminal. At Zulu, we are setting up a database to let us address exactly that need. Would you like me to provide you with details on the program?"

7. Follow-Up With Each of Your Decision Makers.

After your conversations, follow up with each person in your program. Now that you have taken the time to survey these people, you want to make sure they will remember you. Your follow-up package should have 2 components: A custom letter and relevant product information you want each of these people to have.

The custom letter is a short letter, which includes 5 points:

• Thank them for their time.

• Identify a specific useful piece of information that they gave you. This creates a bond to you and makes sure they will remember you and your conversation.

• Share with them some of the ideas that came from your other interviews, and express your company's commitment to address each of these needs.

• If you identified a specific business need during your conversation, reference that and what action you will take to fulfill the businessperson's need.

• Ask the businessperson to call you if you can be of further help.

Add product literature to your package that you think this person might have an interest in. Through your survey process and your follow-up letter, you have basically ensured that your literature will find its way into your decision maker's files for potential use. You want to make sure that this person has enough information about your products when that time comes.

That is it – Seven steps to using surveys as a prospecting tool. Try this very powerful technique. You will be surprised how much you can learn about your prospect's needs to help improve all your business, and you will gain more access to the decision makers you value most.

Helpful Hints

- **Include Board Members on Nonprofit Organizations in Your Survey** – These individuals are looked upon in their community as civic leaders and are natural people to influence other decision makers.

- **Carefully Organize Details in Advance** – Key decision makers are impatient (rightfully so) with individuals who waste their time. Be sure to plan details of your questions and conversations in advance and be as brief as possible.

- **Follow Up With Your Survey Participants** – Decision makers will take special notice of people who remember the courtesy of sending "thank-you" cards or other expressions of appreciation for a busy executives' investment of time with the individual.

Part III

Connecting on the Net

Chapter 11

Communicating in the Virtual Workplace

Virtual versus Real-Time Communications

How time flies – both figuratively and literally. Just ten years ago, e-mail and the Internet were but blips in people's minds. Now, you cannot go to a café in Aruba without seeing a computer connected to the Internet. Last year I was in Charlotte Amalie (St. Thomas, USVI) at a bistro where six computers were in use nonstop with patrons using e-mail and Internet telephony to communicate worldwide.

Today's communication transacts on two distinct levels – virtual and real-time. *Virtual* communication takes place where participants are geographically apart, usually working by computer e-mail and groupware. *Real-time* communication is synchronous, where the sender and receiver are present at the same time.

To prepare for face-to-face meetings, I am often communicating with individuals across the country via e-mail and micro Web sites. I find sharing information on an asynchronous (communication that does not take place in real time) basis via e-mail allows participants I work with in different time zones to contribute bits and pieces to a complete presentation that would take much longer in multiple face-to-face conference room meetings. Jill, in California, (and others in the group just like Jill) can put their two cents into our electronic exchange when a thought comes to mind – whether it is 2:00 a.m. in California or just after lunch in Charlottesville, Virginia.

I can set a time deadline for different activities to take place by different people who possess specific strengths toward the completion of preparing an online presentation. When our online collaboration is complete, we are ready to meet a prospect or customer face-to-face with a finished product that all of us have participated in. Working with others on your own time toward a professional presentation to win new or continuing business – cannot beat that!

Personality and Clarity

Thankfully, colleagues I regularly work with are interested in upholding professional behavior in our communication. That is not always my experience in working with others.

In 1996, an audio technician at a radio station where I was a frequent guest on a radio show decided that he was not happy with the direction our production group was going and sent me a very to-the-point e-mail right after lunch. His clarity was clear, but his personality needed some major improvement.

After reading his e-mail addressed to me and taking a break to "cool-down" from his offensive language, I phoned him to find out what prompted such an electronic outburst. Turns out, he was venting anger about another incident that happened in the office that morning and did not make this clear in his electronic-only communiqué. Had I not phoned this individual, I would have come to the wrong conclusion. I later learned that this audio technician was nicknamed "shark" – for his biting remarks. Other people in the radio station voiced similar experiences to mine about this individual. The way a recipient of an electronic communiqué deciphers a message sent to them is the responsibility of the person sending the message.

You Cannot Beat Face-to-Face

I hear more and more professionals say, "You cannot beat face-to-face meetings" today more than ever. No wonder – virtual communication has to answer the journalist's key questions:

- Who
- What
- When
- Where
- Why
- How
- With whom

(Okay, I editorialized the last point).

Many of us have learned how to apply body language in personal meetings. Few of us have learned to apply "body language" in virtual meetings, and herein lies the conflict. Until you can say to yourself that you are confident you have included answers to the journalist's key questions above in each e-mail (where the tone is presumed businesslike), you are running the risk of being misunderstood and doing more harm to yourself and your company than the "good" you wish to achieve.

Several years ago, when e-commerce was building momentum, many predictions were put forth by business commentators that attendance at trade shows would drop dramatically because people could interact virtually and avoid the distractions of business travel. To some degree, the drop in attendance has occurred because of the ability to interact via computer. Many businesspeople I correspond with constantly, though, now believe there will never be a substitute for face-to-face interaction in building a rapport and trust that can be continued via virtual means. The result that I see today is that trade shows still thrive – just fewer in number.

In a face-to-face meeting, whether you realize it or not, you are communicating answers to the journalistic questions above to those in your presence. This is the reason that you have to **consciously** focus on answering the same questions when using electronic communications.

It is What You Say ... Isn't It?

Yes and no.

In face-to-face and other forms of communication that allow the recipient to hear your voice, often content takes a back seat to tone and delivery. In virtual communication, "content is king."

The interesting activity taking place today is an adjustment by all of us who have become so adept, since childhood, at vocal and body interpretations of others. Virtual communication makes us reflect on our experiences since childhood, sit up and say, "Wait a minute, this is not what I'm used to!" Emoticons (and their derivatives), basic as they are, were invented to add some "emotional" dimension to our virtual communication.

Around and Around We Go ...

From the use of the telegraph clicking out virtual communication and small town hall meetings where everyone met face-to-face in the previous century to the Internet with its e-mail and Web sites today, we are constantly looking for new and better ways to stay in touch and build our connections as efficiently as possible. That is really the key: Staying connected.

As important as "staying connected" in business is, choosing the right media for communication is equally important. Knowing the best means to convey your thoughts and get feedback from others takes planning on the message senders' part. For example, if I wish to interact with Sue about a project we are going to make a presentation on, should I:

- phone her,
- e-mail her,
- make arrangements to meet face-to-face or,
- write and mail her a letter with a return, stamped envelope enclosed?

Whether you choose to communicate *virtually* or in *real-time*, the key is to match the circumstances to your choice of communication, adding your own professional personality that conveys a clear message to your recipients. What turned the world upside down a few years ago with the rapid increase in virtual communication is now moving much closer to the center – using a combination of virtual and real-time to make sure the message is clearly delivered from the sender to the receiver.

Characteristics of Technology-Mediated Communication

We just keep coming up with more ways to communicate with one another. Today, every person feels comfortable with at least one of the six choices listed below that we have available. For example, some of us prefer to leave a voicemail (spoken word) while others like to send an e-mail (written word) and wait (this is a "qualified" wait) for a response.

Several popular methods of virtual communication include:

- The Internet (Web)
- Intranets (for organizational communication)
- Voicemail
- E-mail
- Two-way instant messaging
- Faxes

There is a time and place for each of these methods of communication. For example, the Internet is public, where Intranets are private. Two-way messaging (Blackberry, SkyTel pagers) is directional, where faxes are available for anyone passing by the fax machine to read.

I make every effort to match personal experiences using the six means of communication above with the following four characteristics below for each of the technology-mediated methods for "getting your message across:"

- Personality
- Nonverbals (no face-to-face body language)
- Potential for noise
- Key communications skills required for effective communication

No doubt, each of you has personal stories to share about your communication experiences.

The Internet (Web)

The "personality" of the Internet ranges from formal to extremely informal. Consider the difference between my Web presentations with editors of magazines based in different parts of the country and my pen pal, who is developing a pretty good personal site on GeoCities.

When the Web was gaining momentum a few years ago, everything seemed to be one-way (the Web page owner to whomever looked at the site). Today, Web designers are on private forums with each other trying to help one another build interactivity on their sites. A 12-year old neighbor suggested I include weekly surveys on my site to keep people interested in coming back ("stickiness") – I followed his suggestion.

The Internet (Web) provides each of us with so many color options, font sizes, opportunities to include sound with a URL, screen layouts, on and on, that we have to step back and think carefully about whom we want to attract to our Web creation. If you wish to appeal to business professionals interested in retaining other professionals as vendors (namely you), then the "nonverbal" appeal of your Web site has to take on a business like approach. Contrast this with the MTV Web site where almost any color, font, sound, screen layout and language is acceptable.

Keep the sound on the Web site to a minimum, that is, unless you are sure your audience is on their way to a rock-and-roll concert. The acceptable download time for a start page that I recently heard at an Internet convention was no longer than 12 seconds, using a simple and professional looking "start" page. The Web designers I spoke to in early 2003 mostly said they use 12-, 14-, and 18-point type with a preference toward Times Roman and Arial typestyles.

As with any written presentation, a required key communication skill required is the ability to write clearly and effectively. Equally important for a Web site is the ability to "picture" what your viewers see on the screens that you compose.

Intranets
(Inside Organizational Communication)

Intranets are the modern day "water cooler" in the company break room, though mostly controlled by management. An Intranet is the company's version of Paul Revere riding through town announcing that the British are coming ... only the people living in that town could hear Paul Revere ... Williamsburg was out of earshot at the time. Organizational policies primarily dictate the personality of a company Intranet. Content is "blessed" by management with occasional sprinkling of information from employees allowed. Intranets communicate nonverbal signals much the same as an Internet Web site. The primary difference between the two is that the Intranet is controlled by company policies.

The potential for "noise" with an Intranet lies with interpretation of information. Because an Intranet can set the "tone" for company morale (all employees want to stay in the company information loop), the ability to write clearly and effectively is critical to properly disseminating corporate messages.

Voicemail

Gordon Matthews, inventor of the original software for voicemail, and I had several conversations about his invention. Originally, voicemail was designed to act as a digital answering machine to overcome the repetitive breakage of endless loop in tape machines. Gordon innocently opened Pandora's box.

A recent Ball State University survey of a Fortune 500 company based in the Midwest found that only 7 percent of the messages left on voicemail were returned. My experience is close to this percentage.

The personality of voicemail leaves much to be desired. I used to express my exasperation with people's abuse of this technology until a colleague suggested that I just accept the fact that few people possess basic good manners and not to expect any return calls. Now, I do not expect anyone to return a message I leave on voicemail and am pleasantly surprised when someone does return a call.

Voicemail can be an excellent hybrid of phone call and e-mail as a method of communication ... to those who follow two basic rules:

• When making a call, be prepared in advance to leave an organized message which is no longer than 45 seconds.

• In your message, include the time you called (in the other person's time zone), why you are calling and when you are available to take their call including your phone number with area code (prevents phone tag).

Leaving a message on a digital recorder allows you to express your thoughts using the tone of voice, the volume, pronunciation and speed of speech you choose. You can verbalize the reason for your call and the action you wish the person to take in no more than 45 seconds (some systems have one minute time out mechanisms).

If you properly prepare to leave a voicemail before calling an individual, you will also be ready to speak at an appropriate speed (126 words/minute is normal). Speaking directly toward the microphone on the phone about one inch away from the mouthpiece is optimal. Speak at a speed where someone can write it down.

I feel so strongly about the abuse surrounding voicemail that my message clearly states that I will return calls within four hours (I will change this when going out-of-town to 24 hours). In addition, I promise callers that if I do not return calls within four hours, I will send them $20.00 (this keeps me on my toes as well as waking up the caller). Challenge your callers to leave messages with a firm promise on your part that you will call back in a timely fashion ... and do so – you will then be in the seven percent minority.

E-Mail

I have almost as many true stories to tell about e-mail as I do voicemail ... just a matter of how many days a person has to listen. I can sum up most of the stories into four points:

- Think, think and triple-think about messages you send before you press "send" because the word "private" does not exist online.
- If your message may embarrass your Mom, chances are they will come back to embarrass you. Common sense use of tone and clarity are key to using e-mail.
- E-mail is a great way to bring collaborative thinking from a general sense to an almost specific point ... then you can pick up the phone (or meet face-to-face) and finish the details using your tone and volume of voice.
- If possible, have a Thesaurus, a Dictionary, and a grammatical stylebook handy to help you write professional messages (this is near impossible to do away from your home base). People judge your professional worth by the messages you write.

Two-Way Messaging

I worked with SkyTel when they introduced two-way messaging in the mid-90's. At first, people did not relate well to messaging coming across a large pager. Frequent business travelers were the primary market because they were often away from conventional phones and wanted to stay up to date with colleagues. Now, most travelers have cell phones that carry text messages, so the choices for communication now are more abundant than when two-way messaging was only available through large pagers.

Two-way messaging is appropriate for short, to-the-point messages. I look at "two-way" as a portable "stop-gap" measure designed to keep a decision maker "in the loop" until the decision maker can access other modes of communication to hear the complete story.

Nonverbal cues associated with "two-way" make it necessary to develop excellent writing skills so thoughts can be conveyed in as brief a space as possible. Writing skills for "two-way" are similar to writing skills for e-mail, except the need to focus on brevity.

FAX

Fax messaging has been supplanted, in many ways, by e-mail. Fax communication has many similarities with e-mail because you have to be cognizant that the world could be reading each word you send.

Fax usage was prevalent in overseas communiqués because overseas phone calls were pricey and sending correspondence overseas was expensive and slow. Now, e-mail is worldwide. Any person with an e-mail account and computer printer can accomplish the same thing required by a fax machine a decade ago.

Choose the medium that best communicates your message. I most often use e-mail to set the stage for one-to-one (or small group) collaborations and finish with a phone call or a face-to-face meeting, relying on the other person's voice to guide us both to a mutually beneficial conclusion. For wide area dissemination of information that changes periodically, I rely on the

Web and Intranets ... my "24-hour communiqués." Leaving messages on voicemail fills in the gaps between my written words.

Virtual Teams

A virtual team works across time, geography, organizational hierarchy and cultures. The primary difference between a virtual team and a traditional team is the dimension of space or distance between the individuals.

Employees in the 21st century expect organizational flexibility. Modern teams commonly revolve around technology and knowledge sharing, rather than manufacturing and production.

Advantages of Virtual Teams

Virtual teams can be made up of the best and brightest without regard for geography. A marketing expert can be in Boston, while a product engineering expert can be in Bombay, India.

This new technological team also carries a flatter organizational structure. With a flatter organizational structure, sharing of information can bypass the former chains of command at a central geographical location and go directly to those who can readily influence the final decision on the company's product or service.

Starting a Virtual Team

Ideally, a person with leadership qualities should initiate a team. Leadership qualities that the coordinator needs to possess in order to build an effective team include:

- Humility (lack of arrogance)

- Sensitivity to the strengths and weaknesses of each team member

- Fairness to all members

- Organizational skills

- Strong work ethic

The leader should organize a basic framework for the virtual team with input from team members, including:

- Mission and Objectives of the team.

- Policies and Procedures the team expects from one another (how often to check and respond to e-mail and voicemail, expectation of timeliness, how to resolve personal differences, how to conclude a project online together).

- Periodic events to build team cohesiveness (exchanging "bios," create a "forum", distribute a map graphic showing where each team member resides).

Communicating as a Team

Once you have formed your virtual team, an understanding needs to take place on how members will communicate with one another. Team communication is a collaborative effort.

Once again, the team leader needs to take responsibility for making sure that each team member has a fair chance of making a contribution to the team. The main disadvantage of a team of diverse "experts" coming together to solve a common issue is that the team members are dependent upon one another for knowledge and information. Take one team member out of the group (say, a production manager) and the human resource manager and marketing manager cannot say for sure if a product can be realistically manufactured (because of the absence of the production manager).

You Need it When?

For any team meeting, there are four possibilities for means of interacting:

- Same Time, Same Place (face-to-face, videoconferencing)

- Different Time, Same Place (shift work, reviewing typewritten drafts)

- Same Time, Different Place (telephone)

- Different Time, Different Place (e-mail, voicemail)

The psychological distance moves from being close in "Same Time, Same Place" to remote in "Different Time, Different Place."

Cross-Border Communication

Virtual teaming creates a loss of informal communication, where people meet in the break room or in the hall on the way to the elevator, etc. This is particularly acute when collaboration is taking place across geographical borders. The difference in time zones, individual cultures, cultural practices and semantics of the English language can create havoc if there is not a framework laid out in the beginning by the team leader.

For example, Americans have phrases for different sizes of apartments ("efficiency" size does not have a separate bedroom). The British word for an apartment without a separate bedroom is "flat" ... quite a difference.

Imagine what confusion can occur if you are talking about shipping heavy machinery from Charleston, SC, to Southampton, U.K., without a firm grip on the semantics of questionable words. A purchasing agent in the U.K. could be asking the company team for a John Deere Tractor to complete a construction project and receive a John Deere Bulldozer instead ... quite an expensive snafu due to cross-cultural semantics.

International time zones can create communication difficulties in virtual teams (unless addressed and accepted in the beginning). For example, two members of a team on the East

Coast of America can have an urgent need for information within two hours of posting an e-mail at 3 p.m. Eastern Time. Two team members having the required information are located in Western Europe five to six hours later in the day (8-9 p.m.) and understandably not at the office to respond. As a result of the time zone difference, information is received in America at 4 a.m. East Coast time the next day.

Virtual teams can work – if properly led. A team leader who is knowledgeable about coordinating a diverse group of individuals in different geographical locations can bring the knowledge of each team member to a group dynamic not possible by members acting alone.

Whether a company is virtual, virtual with bricks, or bricks, certain functions stay the same:

- **Marketing and Sales** – You have to identify who is most likely to buy your product, build a communication program to get the message to this audience and ask for the signature on the dotted line.

- **Finance and Accounting** – You have to get the money in (Finance) while you are circulating and percolating the money out (Accounting).

- **Administration (including purchasing)** – You have to have a system for keeping all the pieces of the business working together smoothly. I feverishly work building "systems" that operate smoothly and continually try to improve.

- **Human Resources** – People are the most important asset a business has. Prospects and customers constantly decide whom to do business with based on a trust they have in certain company personnel. Ask Arthur Andersen, WorldCom, and Tyco where their former customers are.

- **Technology** – Chief Information Officers never had to read so much to keep up to date. Younger, promising employees gravitate to the company that offers them the best opportunity to work around the newest technology. I know from recruiting.

- **Research and Development** – Historically, companies that invest heavily in R&D are leaders in their fields (assuming all other functions are performing well). R&D amounts to deciding what your company can produce (whether goods or services) the most profitably that the largest audience is likely to buy.

To Be or Not To Be (Online)

A simple question concerning your business: "Should I be just virtual, virtual brick, or just brick?" The answer depends on the type of business you operate.

For example, I have never seen livery stables (place to keep horses) as just virtual. Livery stables make sense as a virtual-brick operation because many people who look for quality boarding for their horse are also Internet savvy. You produce "special reports" (presentation of information longer than 5 pages and shorter than 50 pages). A business selling "special reports" lends itself to just virtual because the overhead for a local brick-and-mortar store is too high to support sales of information packages that can be automatically delivered anywhere in the world from a small office with an Internet connection. You operate a local restaurant that has built up a wonderful reputation over the years for having a great atmosphere and delicious food. Likely, the "just-brick" choice would fit.

Helpful Hints

- Communication with business colleagues has forever changed with the Internet and e-mail ... forward-thinking businesspeople are working hard to find the right combination of virtual and real-time interaction to maximize productivity.

- Deciphering hidden meanings in face-to-face meetings has long been known ... deciphering virtual communication meanings is largely an uncharted territory and still under development.

- Each individual can excel in business when they find their right combination of virtual and real-time communication. Ideal mixtures of the two are different for each businessperson.

- You can build customer loyalty when you utilize the modes of communication that your individual buyers feel most comfortable with. For example, one buyer may only communicate via e-mail and another buyer prefers to talk over lunch.

- Virtual communication breaks down geographic borders and allows you to assemble a specialized team from the highest qualified personnel anywhere in the world.

Chapter 12

Staying Connected With E-mail

Written Communication Will Never Be the Same

If you want to give your online marketing a personal touch, create a Web community and position yourself in the center of it. Brand yourself using e-mail.

Greg Landry, an exercise physiologist, crunched the marketing numbers and immediately saw the writing on the wall. Composing, printing, and mailing a four-page weekly newsletter to 14,000 recipients would run about $5,000 per issue. Sending it out as an electronic magazine – or e-zine – would drop the cost from several days of his time to one month's hosting service fee for a fraction of the cost.

It was not a tough decision. Landry now gets on his electronic soapbox each week, spreading the word about his health and nutrition enterprise and branding himself as an authority – all at a very low cost.

"This is heaven for a marketer," says Landry from his Wilmington, N.C. office. He parlays the exposure from his "Fitness, Health & Weight Loss" e-zine to sell his self-published book, *The Metabolism System*. He is positioning himself at the center of a community, and he is doing so without breaking the bank – or his back.

The Internet has changed the face of marketing, but not just in terms of providing low-cost access to potential customers. If you are an entrepreneur with a computer, an Internet account, and a penchant for writing, you can create an online newsletter that helps build brand awareness for both your product and yourself. "The newsletter gives me expert status automatically," says

Landry, who holds a master's degree in exercise physiology. "Whether you are an expert or not, you become one."

Landry's e-zine debuted in January 1995, when he sent it to 30 friends. Today he e-mails to more than 18,000 subscribers and the list is growing monthly.

What draws Web surfers in? Content that is fresh, frequent and pertinent to the audience, says Adam Boettiger, Vice President of Business Development with Eyescream Interactive, a Portland, Oregon, Internet advertising agency, and creator of the Internet Advertising Discussion List. Boettiger urges prospective expert entrepreneurs to research the market to determine what information already exists and what kind of information is lacking. Write a business plan to help you target your audience and refine your offering. Choose a few trustworthy people and send them some beta samples so you can hear what they have to say about everything – your content, design elements, tone and even the disclaimer. Here are a few more tips.

Make it topical. Keep your e-zine pertinent to your readers; make it something they anticipate. Desire by your readers will help create buzz. To foster growth, Boettiger frankly asks recipients to forward his e-zine to anyone they think might benefit from it. "Most of the growth has been by word of mouth," he says. Post your e-zine to online directories of e-zines, lists and discussion groups. Sites include http://www.liszt.com and http://www.meer.net/~johnl/e-zine-list (which is no longer being maintained but looking for volunteers).

For Landry, the future is energizing. He plans to brand Fitness, Health & Weight Loss as the centerpiece of a growing business. Along with his e-zine, Web site, book and resulting consultations, he is developing teleconferencing, new health food products and audiotapes. His Webmaster is designing a ticker tape applet that visitors can add to their own Web sites to bring a fitness tip of the day.

All of these features and all of this hype, he is fully aware, originate from a personal investment in some time and money. "You're exposing yourself to so many people at so little cost," he says. "You can't beat it."

Think Relevant Marketing

Marketers are masters of marketing to large groups because marketing to small groups has been too costly. With e-mail, it is possible to micro market. For example:

- A retailer can cement relationships with its best customers by delivering a special offer only to them and electronically connecting them to a private area on its Web site to take advantage of the promotion.

- A cruise line with excess capacity can execute an e-mail campaign that offers special discounts to the line's most frequent customers in time to fill empty cabins.

- A cataloger can move low-inventory items by e-mailing several thousand or even a few hundred customers and still control costs enough for an acceptable profit margin. Such just-in-time, pinpoint marketing protects the bottom line, builds customer loyalty and avoids polluting a customer list with margin-busting offers.

One-to-One Marketing

E-mail provides an innovative way to maximize return on one of a company's most important assets, its customers. By providing more and better information about individuals' responses and buying patterns, e-mail technology enables marketers to fine-tune offers in even the largest campaigns down to the one-on-one level.

For instance, by embedding several response links or electronic connections to the marketer's Web site in an e-mail promotion, marketers can determine who responds to a solicitation and what aspect of the offer stimulated their response. This insight is as readily obtained in a mailing of 5,000 messages as it is in a mailing of 5 million.

Consider a Web music retailer that collects e-mail addresses from site visitors. The retailer may construct an e-mailing that highlights its latest additions in each music category. Embedded hotlinks can let the consumer listen to a preview of a CD in each music category. Even if the prospects did not buy, consumers who listened to the latest jazz offering have indicated an interest in jazz. The next time this music retailer contacts that consumer it will be to tell them about new jazz offerings.

By integrating e-mail marketing results into a database, marketers archive key information about every message recipient. The resulting database will identify who was most motivated by discounts, rebates and special offers; who was the most interested in hearing about the latest merchandise; and who did not respond and probably needs a different approach. In future mailings, the marketer can use this intelligence to create a stronger dialogue with each customer.

Through a database approach, the Web environment also can be personalized, making it easier for customers to order. For example, as part of subscription renewal efforts, publications can bring subscribers to a Web site where their order form information is already pre-filled. The consumer can simply review the information and click a "Yes, bill me" field or enter his or her credit card information. Customized Web display features available through some of the more advanced e-mail delivery systems can improve response rates dramatically.

Consider this: An Acxiom/Bigfoot e-mail test generated a 1.5 percent response rate within an hour and a final response rate of 20.7 percent. In other campaigns, e-mail response rates have reached 56 percent in fewer than two days.

E-mail Linking Messages

Link e-mail with Web content. Embed hot links in the message that will make it easy for the reader to visit the marketer's Web site. Keep initial mailings short and to the point. Recipients are reading these messages on their computer monitors and web-enabled phones. Employ message personalization and customization when possible. Analyze each call to action or link in a mailing to determine what works and what does not, and archive that knowledge in your marketing database. Use your brand equity. Include your company name as the sender of the message. This distinguishes you from the anonymous spammers. Give a compelling reason to open or read the message in the header or subject line.

Keep it simple. For now, you should deliver only text e-mail messages with embedded hot links because only about 60 percent of e-mail recipients can read HTML mail. Use the power of interactivity. Embed multiple calls to action in the e-mail message offering recipients several choices or hot links. Multiple offers increase the probability of a sale and generate valuable information that can then be appended back to your database.

Tips For Handling Customer Service Using E-Mail

Many companies are constructing Web sites designed to attract customers, only to find themselves swamped with e-mails they are not prepared to respond to efficiently or effectively. By the end of 2002, there were 415 million e-mail addresses – more than one per person – in the United States, according to the trade publication, *Messaging Online*. The figure represents a 73 percent increase in a year. Here are 14 tips for businesses looking for ways to communicate effectively with customers on the Net.

1. **Respond Efficiently**
    Customers and prospects expect a response to their e-mails between 24 and 48 hours after contact. Just as you would not ask a customer to hold on the phone for 20 minutes, you should not expect a person to wait more than two days for an e-mail response.

2. **Know Your Netiquette**
    Be careful not to offend the writer, as specific rules apply when writing in cyberspace. For example, never use all caps unless you want to be perceived as screaming. Use asterisks around a word to emphasize a point. On the Web, "you won't be judged by the color of your skin, eyes or hair, your weight, your age or your clothing," author Virginia Shea says in her rules of "Netiquette," which are posted online at **www.in.on.ca/tutorial/netiquette.html**. "You will, however, be judged by the quality of your writing."

    The solution? Re-read your e-mail, not only for mistakes but also for impetuous words, says Eric Arnum, editor of *Messaging Online*.

3. **Staff Appropriately**
   Be prepared for out-of-the-ordinary e-mail spikes – especially following a high-profile promotion or new advertising campaign. During these times you can expect large volumes of e-mails, so you should have the systems in place to be able to respond in a timely fashion.

4. **Write for Your Reader**
   No one wants to receive a form letter and it is even worse to receive form e-mail. Tailor your responses, adopting the tone used by your customer. For example, be formal if the message is formal and relaxed if the e-mail is casual.

5. **Keep a Sense of Humor**
   Use humor sparingly in the professional environment. Try to keep your response light without becoming unprofessional.

6. **Capture Your Company's Image**
   Project your company's image in your responses. Whether your company is a high-profile athletic shoe manufacturer or PCS phone service provider, it has an image brought to the marketplace through advertising, marketing and other collateral that should be integrated into your e-mail messages.

7. **Concentrate on Your Core Business**
   You may be experimenting with new ideas on the Internet, but experimenting with your customer service is dangerous. The best solution is to focus on what your business does best and outsource the rest.

8. **Write Well**
   Just as your customers like to hear a well-spoken representative on the phone, they also want to receive a well-written and creative e-mail message. When selecting cyber reps (your company representatives exclusively communicating via the Internet), remember that they require a different skill set than telephone representatives, and the ability to write well is a necessary skill.

9. **Be Prepared for Legal Issues**
   Remember each e-mail is the same as a written document. Be sure to train your employees corresponding via e-mail to be sensitive to legal issues.

10. **Complement Other Mediums**
    The telephone, Internet and U.S. mail are tools that should complement each other, each reaching a targeted audience and each equal in importance. Just as you would not ignore a phone call or a letter from a customer, you should not neglect to respond to e-mails efficiently.

11. **Develop and Post a Privacy Policy**
    Posting a privacy policy greatly boosts response rates. Place yours prominently on your Web site and include a comprehensive description of your e-mail marketing practices, as well as a clear statement of how customer information will and will not be used.

    To make sure this policy is both visible and accessible, put links to it on your home page and in any e-mails you send to customers. Many customers will never read the policy at all. Seeing it (or at least references to it) every time they have contact with you reassures them that you will do the right thing with their data.

12. **Guarantee that Personal Information is Secure**
    Create secure customer profile pages. If confidential information about customers is available on a sign-up form, or profile page, make sure it is password protected. Explain to your customers when they enroll how passwords guarantee that they will be the only ones (other than you) who will ever have access to their password data.

13. **Get to the Point**
    Always write concise, descriptive subject lines for your customer communications. Because you often know the interests of your customers, it can be easy to craft a message that may be of interest to them. For example, if you know your audience tends to own a personal digital assistant such as a Palm Pilot, send out an e-mail with the subject line, "Extend the battery life of your Palm XV", or "Sneak preview: A new Palm tool to help you stay

organized." If you target your message to your audience, more customers are likely to read and respond to your messages, and your unsubscribe rates should remain low.

14. **Solicit Feedback**
E-mail allows you to easily find out from your customers what they think your company is doing right and where you still have to improve. Take full advantage of this opportunity by constantly inviting and encouraging customers to communicate with you. Establish an online suggestion box or message posting location for your Web site. Set up a dedicated e-mail address so customers can give you immediate feedback that way, too. Reply to each message within 24 hours, if possible. When you get helpful feedback, do something about it. If you make a significant change to your policy based on a customer suggestion, let them know. Customers who know that you are listening to them will quickly become your advocates.

E-mail and the Web are almost limitless channels for reaching businesses and consumers. The future is here for interactive marketing, and the medium for capturing its opportunity is e-mail.

Helpful Hints

- **Have language reference materials nearby** – When you are composing e-mail messages, have a thesaurus, dictionary and other word-usage references nearby because the way you write your e-mail reflects your inner thoughts to the outer world.

- **E-mail newsletter** – Begin an e-mail newsletter including recipients in your target audience who accept your invitation to provide them with helpful information. One newsletter every two to four weeks works well for you to brand yourself, and for recipients to continue inviting you into their e-mail inbox.

- **Professional software** – Be sure to use professional messaging software and constantly test messages by sending tests to yourself first before you e-mail communiqués to your entire recipient list.

- **Commit to timely response** – I make it my policy to respond to e-mails needing a response within 48 hours, usually within four hours.

Chapter 13

Connecting People via the Web

E-mail, voice mail, Internet, fiber optics, satellites, video conferencing – every advancement in technology is designed to help us connect with each other better, faster and cheaper. Information without effective communication, however, is mere data. After all, developing business is about people.

The telephone, Internet and U.S. mail are tools that should complement each other, each reaching a targeted audience and each equal in importance.

As you begin to think about your Web site as a business tool, it is tempting to get drawn into a sense of urgency and to rush your approach with aggressive sales techniques. Web culture, however, frowns on this "hard sell" approach. The Web was originally designed by and for non-commercial organizations and has been advanced by individuals wanting to commercially connect. In order to catch the attention and approval of a businessperson, it is still more acceptable to give something away on your site. In fact, it is common to hear the adage "information wants to be free" used as a password to Web wisdom. If you want to build relationships with Web businesspeople, give them something they value before you turn their attention to your sales presentation.

The important thing about the free content you provide is that it must be valuable to the prospect. If it is information, it should answer the questions prospects actually ask. It should give them pointers to more information. If it is entertainment, it should be interesting and engaging. If it is some form of product, it should be something that you expect they can use. In any case, your site should constantly be evolving so those customers have a reason to come back again and again.

Two Examples of Giving Away Entertainment are...

Movie studios put up clips, pictures, descriptions and other teasers to encourage you to attend the films when they play at "a theater near you." Dilbert cartoons on the Web encourage the popularity of the strip and promote the Dilbert books and merchandise.

Two Examples of Giving Away Product are...

Microsoft giving away the Web browser, Internet Explorer, in hopes of selling operating systems and authoring tools.

Paint Shop Pro gives away their program for trial use and asks users to purchase it after 30 days. They are hopeful that users will decide to purchase the product and also buy their other products.

An Example of Giving Away Information is Where...

Novell was famous in the early days of the Web because they put their entire documentation collection on the Web while other companies had only a page or two. Novell accomplished this by using SGML, the Standard Generalized Markup Language. SGML allows you to manage your Web documents at a level above HTML (the standard format for documents on the Web).

Another form of interactivity is achieved through fill-in forms. An example of this is available at the Toronto Dominion Bank's site. They let consumers enter data on how much money they would like to have when they retire, and the server returns calculations about the required level of annual contributions. Not only does this site provide information through interactions with the customer, it provides customers with information about themselves. This type of interaction is implemented through CGI scripts. CGI scripts run on a server and are visible in the browser only as forms and form results.

Some sites use more advanced forms of interactivity such as virtual worlds and Java. For now, some of your audience will not have a browser, which supports these more advanced forms. Watch carefully, though, technologies that are futuristic today will be ancient history before you know it!

First we discussed providing static information for customers. Then we discussed ways of having them interact with documents and software through interactivity. Creating a personal relationship with consumers is to have them communicate with actual people.

The simplest way to encourage personal communication is to provide simple mechanisms for them to reach you: An e-mail address, phone number, etc. It is critical that when they make this important step of trying to contact you, someone replies immediately. I try to respond within two hours and no later than 48 hours to every e-mail I receive requiring a reply. Just as you do not let phone messages sit in voice mail for days, do not allow an e-mail message to stay in your inbox too long. Consumers will immediately infer that you are not interested in them or in their business. It is especially important to solicit feedback on your Web site and your Web services. You can use this feedback to improve your site and make it a better reflection of your customers' needs. Your prompt response also shows customers you are listening to them and trying to meet their needs.

One example of the effective use of combined information, interaction and response can be seen when Honda launched the 1996 Acura TL series on their Web site by allowing viewers to call up technical specifications, photographs, and details on the nearest dealer. Within hours of requesting more information, the consumer received a call from a dealer.

Consider MacLean's. This magazine went online with CompuServe. Accessible to more than 2 million CompuServe subscribers globally, including 100,000 in Canada, MacLean's offers a package to advertisers for $25,000 for 3 months, which includes up to 12 screens with 6 high-resolution graphics. Users select a "Promotions and Products" icon to see electronic brochures, offers and ways of getting more information. Users can also browse stories and some photos from the current issue of MacLean's, search issues back to 1989, read editor's picks of stories back to 1929, read background information too long for traditional publications, send letters, subscribe, chat with staff, other subscribers, or special guests.

An especially important form of feedback is the user-to-user feedback provided by forum software like HyperNews or chat software like WebChat. With this software, users can actually build up a sense of community among themselves and you. You can also bring in guest speakers to educate and stimulate the users.

Customer service personnel can be directly linked to Web users at your Web site directly, linked via such services as LivePerson.com and HelpDesk.com. Web call centers are beginning to replace traditional telemarketing customer service centers as the preferred method prospects and customers communicate with a company.

The end goal is a win-win situation. Customers are happy because their concerns and comments are heard and a response is received. You can more easily sell your products and services to them because you know what they want and have made them feel comfortable with you.

Linking

Providing links to other related resources is an easy way to boost the information value of your Web site. It is also a good way to show your visitors that you are as interested in serving their needs as in tooting your own horn. Many Web sites now have a "related resources" or "other cool sites" department that offers collections of links to other places. In fact, some of the most visited Web sites are essentially collections of links, like the Yahoo directory.

Every link you add to your site, though, is a doorway to another location, an escape hatch that moves the visitor out of your information space and into another. Once visitors make that escape, they may not return to your site at all. So while you want to help your visitors find related resources, you do not want to show them the exit to your site before you have a chance to show your own stuff. Here are five strategies for including links in your Web site.

1.   Do not put links on your home page.

Give visitors a chance to see what you are offering before showing them doorways to other sites. If you offer links, put them on pages that are nested at least one level below the home page in your Web site, so visitors will be exposed to at least some of your own information before they can head for the door. It is like putting the milk at the back of the supermarket.

2. **Check out each link yourself before including it.**

    It is easy to grab a cool sounding URL out of an Internet magazine or from a discussion group post, but you should always check out the resource yourself before including it. The URL may be wrong, or the site may contain material that is detrimental to your own marketing efforts.

3. **Link to sites that augment, rather than compete with, the information you are offering.**

    Look for sites that offer more detail about a subject your site covers.

4. **Skip the "cool" site links.**

    Do not provide links to sites that do not directly relate to what you are offering. Inviting somebody to visit a site with games, puzzles, or cool graphics or video just distracts them from the subject they were focused on when they chose to view your site originally. It is hard enough to hold someone's attention without inviting your visitors into an unrelated detour.

5. **Ask for reciprocal links.**

    When you include a link to another site, let that site's owner know and ask for a link from their site back to your site. Visitors can always navigate back to your site using their browser's navigation buttons, but it will not hurt to remind them by having a link on other sites, too.

    This brings me to another point...

Proactive Internet Marketing

The problem with too many Internet marketing strategies is that they depend on visitors voluntarily coming back to a Web site. I call this "Inbound Marketing Strategies." I believe that no Internet marketing strategy is complete unless it incorporates both an Inbound and an Outbound Marketing Strategy. An outbound marketing strategy refers to any technique on the Internet that is proactive and takes you to the customer, rather than being inactive, waiting for the customer to come to you. Good examples of "Outbound Marketing Strategies" include:

* Reminder Notices
* Profiled Information Streams
* E-mail Newsletters (to your established list)
* Discussion List Participation
* Online Conferences

Reminder Notices

Reminder notices typically highlight activities about your company, new announcements, highlights about additions to your Web site, specific URLs where detailed information can be found, etc.

For example, C/Net and HotWired both use reminder notices to maintain visibility with their readers. C/Net has over 250,000 people on their mailing list and HotWired probably has over 150,000 people on their distribution list. I personally subscribe to both lists, but never visit the Web site unless there is something specific in their reminder notice that is of interest to me. I am certain these distribution lists have a major impact on driving traffic to their respective Web sites.

Profiled Information Streams

"Profiled Information Streams" refers to customized information, which is sent to each subscriber, based on his or her own personal information needs. Each customer creates a "profile" of the kind of information they seek. Then, on an ongoing basis, they receive any information which meets their specific profile.

Another approach is most relevant when a company has a wide range of offerings and customers require a great deal of information on an ongoing basis. IBM has implemented this type of profiling capability where customers can subscribe to information regarding specific products, services and technologies.

E-mail newsletters

One major advantage of outbound strategies via e-mail is that almost 100 percent of Internet users have e-mail access. However, probably only about 60 percent of users have access to the Web, which is the backbone to most Internet, inbound strategies. The key to a viable e-mail newsletter is that it must be totally based on the prospect's desire to receive this type of information. Newsletters can act as an extension to the Web site with the objectives of strengthening your brand image, increasing sales, and creating a sense of community with their readers.

For example, almost a year ago, I found a Web site that sells lobster called "Lobster Direct." (They are at http://www.lobsterdirect.com and I am not affiliated with them in any way). Since it was an interesting site, I added it to my bookmarks. However, I have never been back to the site (Who has the time?). Although I have not placed an order yet, I have been positively influenced by the company, and will likely place an order this year. There are "Jokes" and "Lobster Tales" sections where they poke fun at themselves (i.e., Canadian Maritimers). They have a drawing every month for a free lobster (which keeps me from unsubscribing). They try to interact with their customers through lobster-related, fun-filled surveys. They provide lobster recipes, and of course, they try to sell me some lobster.

Discussion List Participation

For discussion lists to be successful, the list members must be part of your target market. You need to add value to the list through direct participation with the group. Your signature file needs to be relevant and appropriate for the type of group participation. This approach will keep your name and company in front of your target market on a regular basis.

Online Conferences

By becoming a speaker in an online conference, you get a chance to show people what you know and how you can help them. If you have some expertise that may be of interest to lots of online subscribers, you may be able to schedule a special online conference. Such conferences are usually promoted in the opening or closing screen of a service, such as America Online. If your expertise is subject specific, you may be able to schedule a conference on a particular forum or special interest group and promote it just within that group. You can leverage your online conference by selecting a few questions and answers from the text record of the conference proceedings and publishing them as a Q&A document.

Using Technology For Delivering Live Web Presentations

Web presentation software and services eliminate the need to travel to deliver a live presentation. Plus, presenting via the Web offers advantages that face-to-face presentations do not – namely, unique ways to interact with your audience and archive the results for later retrieval. That is the good news. The bad news is that the number of software and service offerings in today's constantly changing marketplace is a bit overwhelming.

Three Ways to Present via the Web

Web presentation products and services fall into three primary categories:

1. Basic Web presentation software

These programs allow you to publish simple HTML presentations to a Web server (usually by converting existing slideshows), but their live presentation capabilities are limited. For example, they do not include the ability to synchronize live audio, display text transcripts of the presenter's words, or capture audience interaction.

Each of the major presentation software packages (Microsoft PowerPoint, Lotus Freelance Graphics, Corel Presentations and Astound) as well as niche digital-photo presentation products (such as InMedia Slides & Sound Plus and MetaCreations MetaShow) include a wizard that walks you through the process of converting your existing presentations into HTML files. Most convert your slides to a series of .gif or .jpeg images and add navigation buttons for forward/backward viewing, which eliminates all sound and animation. If you want the audience to experience all the movement you have added to your presentation, the viewer typically has to download a specific plug-in – but even then it is nearly impossible to deliver live presentations.

At the high end of this category are SPC Active Presenter, Astound Dynamite, Microsoft NetShow and MatchWare Mediator. These tools are either specifically or partly designed for producing Web presentations with movement and audio, but fall short of the tightly integrated presentation capabilities offered by the Webcasting tools in the next category.

2. Webcasting software

These software programs make it easy to combine slides, audio, video and animation into seamless presentations, then broadcast them live over the Web to large groups of people. Some Webcasting tools also offer sophisticated features such as text transcripts of the presenter's words, polling, messaging, virtual chat rooms, a shared whiteboard and robust archiving.

Webcasting programs typically consist of two parts – a special wizard that helps you gather various forms of content into one broadcast file (sometimes called a builder) and server software that manages the flow of content, messages, polls and interactivity during a live broadcast.

Some of the most exciting new programs in this category include Contigo Itinerary, Netpodium Interactive Broadcasting Suite, PlaceWare Conference Center, Eloquent Presenter! and Starlight Networks StarLive! Each makes it possible to broadcast multimedia rich presentations to hundreds of participants. Once the Webcast is complete, the entire presentation can be archived on a dedicated URL and viewed later by people who could not make the live broadcast. Another option is to export the Webcast to CD-ROM for distribution or Adobe .pdf file.

3. Webcasting services

If you want someone else to invest in all the software, hardware, personnel and high-speed Internet connections necessary for a top-notch Web presentation, a Webcasting service provider is the answer. These service bureaus also provide coaching sessions and media preparation services. They will even take care of audience invitations and archive your presentation for later viewing. Hiring a Webcast service provider is expensive – you can expect to pay several thousand dollars for a simple show and up to $50,000 for a full-fledged multimedia event – but it is by far the easiest way to present on the Web.

Webcasting service providers will take your PowerPoint presentation and add a variety of interactive features, or they will work with you to create a Webcast from scratch. Some even have full-service production studios outfitted with professional audiovisual equipment. Each offers various levels of service, allowing you to pick and choose how fancy you want to get and still stay within your budget. Some of the top Webcasting service bureaus include Broadcast.com (formerly AudioNet), Talkpoint Communications, E.N.E.N., E-Conference, and iMeet.

Design Your Site With Women in Mind
How to attract them and keep them as customers for a long-term business relationship

Women are accustomed to creative merchandising in the catalog and retail environment, and there is no reason to expect that they would not desire a similar experience online. It may be argued that the online environment needs to be even more dynamic if it is to encourage women to shop online.

Women, who five years ago made up fewer than 10 percent of online users, are reported by Nielsen to be more than 50 percent of today's online audience. Since women account for about 70 percent of all retail purchases, online merchants must market their merchandise and services to meet and exceed their expectations.

It will be wise for merchants to take note of a recent Giftware News study detailing women's top complaints about shopping. Many of these complaints are driving forces that are leading shoppers in general and women in particular to migrate to the Web.

From a selection standpoint, many women said they could not find what they were looking for and were confused by the proliferation of products. Even when they do locate the item, many complained that they could not find knowledgeable salespeople or clear and accurate pricing or sales information.

Women also called the checkout process too time consuming. Many expressed a desire for home delivery, particularly for everyday products from stores that are too far away, they said. Also, childcare and personal safety were concerns. No wonder this time-starved segment is an ideal target for online marketers. Here are five suggestions for improving your online marketing efforts with women in mind:

1. **Understand the nature of your shopper and design your site around those needs.**

   As an example, if your customers constantly look for specific merchandise – as many women do – rather than browse, it is best to make the search function available on the homepage. If your customers do browse and you want to maximize impulse purchases, make sure the "buy" function is available on all product screens. Be straightforward in delivering the message. Women are less enamored by the bells and whistles and more interested in the efficiency you provide. Be sensitive to time constraints by making your site easy to navigate and quick to download. Offer products that can be sold online that are important to women's lifestyles. The more sophisticated, expensive and unfamiliar the product, the more likely the consumer will want to see it firsthand. Everyday goods or replenishment items, such as cosmetics or pantyhose, can be sold with a picture and a description.

   Enhance the user experience by including value-added services. Examples include such customer service oriented programs as gift registry or reminder programs. Personal shopper services allow the customer to take control by telling you what they want. You can then follow up with personalized e-mails telling them that their size is now in stock or that their favorite designer has a new line. Offer impulse buys, up sells and related goods. The Limited Express Web site has a mix-and-match function that shows which shirts go with which skirts and pants. You also might suggest related accessories such as belts, shoes or scarves. If your site recognizes past customers, tap into their buying history and suggest new or related merchandise.

2. **Build "community" within your site.**

   Alleviate the impersonal nature of the Web by inviting feedback via e-mail or chat opportunities with other customers through a chat board.

3. **Make strategic alliances with content sites oriented to the women you want to reach.**

   Take advantage of a partner's online development skills to create more of a one-stop resource within your merchant environment. Articles, co-branded chat rooms or bulletin boards and joint promotions are among the possibilities. This will encourage longer site visits and more repeat traffic as customers gain a feeling they are part of your online community.

4. **Listen to women's needs and learn more about your customers' interests.**

   Continually rebuild and update your site based on feedback and results. If women's outerwear is selling but accessories are suffering, add more outerwear and tinker with accessory offers. If accessories still will not sell, try a new category. Pay attention to e-mail requests and complaints. Change your merchandise and add new lines to keep things fresh.

5. **Online merchants must deliver better value than can be found at retail while serving up the best in what technology can offer.**

   As women continue to find products they desire in an atmosphere where they are comfortable, they will undoubtedly be a major part of this new electronic shopping channel.

   You can summarize Web-based communications by the slogan, "Success is all about making the right connections."

Helpful Hints

- **Web relations** – This can be a new job title. Think about building relationships on the Web. Think interactivity.

- **Study the Web sites of big companies** – Big companies typically commit major resources to keeping their brand and image attractive. Large companies can stimulate ideas for you to use in your Web site.

- **Study small creative companies** – I learn as much of what to do as often as what not to do reviewing ad agency, public relations and other service-type creative company Web sites.

- **Visit computer stores and Internet trade shows** – Keep up with the latest trends in Web products and services ... your audience will be glad you do.

- **Professional and Unique** – You can never go wrong combining professionalism with uniqueness.

Part IV

Connecting with the Written Word

Chapter 14

"Connecting" Introductory Note

Picture this: I am alone in Dallas, Texas, in 1983 with a commission sales job, no contacts and bills to pay. Thankfully, the sales manager of the company where I worked and I were very compatible.

Prospecting for new customers in the early 80's was still based on wearing out a new pair of shoes every two months, canvassing the high rise buildings, telephoning 50 companies each day and attending networking events hoping to meet a decision maker who allows themselves to be seen in public. For almost two years, I worked hard, long hours trying to uncover decision makers that could say, "yes" to an order. Hard as I worked, none of the tried-and-true methods was working for me.

One Friday afternoon, as I was driving home discouraged about the lack of business activity during the week, I passed a retail store selling stationery products. "What an idea," I thought. "All I'm doing now is spending my time and money trying to personally reach 'the unreachable' decision maker face-to-face, so why not try a new method no one has suggested to me yet ... send a personalized note to each prospect?"

Browsing the stationery store that afternoon, I saw many options of letters and envelopes from which to choose. I thought about the cards and envelopes I received at the office. Which formats caught my attention? Which shapes and sizes got the "heave-ho" into the trash. My conclusion narrowed to cards and notes that were business like, professional and unique. With this in mind, the choices were drastically reduced.

The store attendant brought a coordinated stationery package to my attention that was perfect. The stationery was too small to fit in the standard #10 business envelope and the matching envelopes had an attractive logo embossed on the flap. I bought two packages for a total of 50 notes and envelopes. My plan was to mail a small, personal and business-like, note to each of the top 30 key decision makers that had been so elusive to me for so long. The decision makers on my "Top 30" list included:

- Presidents of small companies in Dallas
- Senior-level executives of large corporations in Dallas

In 1983, laser printers and personal computers were not on every desktop, so I hand typed all 30 notes and envelopes over the two-day weekend. While I was typing, I kept thinking to myself that if this idea did not work, I would seek other employment within the month. Every note and every envelope was checked and double-checked for accuracy and appearance.

Monday morning, on the way to the office, I held my breath and dropped the 30 notes in the mailbox. All the notes were addressed to companies in Dallas so I had confidence that each envelope would reach the intended decision maker no later than Wednesday afternoon. As I saw people in the office during the first part of the week, I did not say that I had done anything different over the weekend because I did not know whether my idea would generate even a ripple effect in business.

On Thursday afternoon, I held my breath again and began to follow up by phone from my office with my "Top 30." What did I have to lose except several hours spent on perfecting the notes and a few dollars in postage? What happened next completely took me by surprise.

My follow-up script for each letter via telephone went something like this:

> "Hi (person who answered the phone), this is Michael McCann with (my company name). I am calling to add a brief voice to the small blue note that I mailed to ('Top 30' name) on Monday. Is he/she available?"

Without exception, each phone call was forwarded to the next level closer to the decision maker. I often recited this same script to two or more assistants before connecting with the decision maker's personal assistant. With the "Top 30's" personal assistant, I again repeated the same script.

After mailing 30 short, business-like notes, I spoke with 25 hard-to-reach decision makers. From these 25 decision makers, I closed 18 large sales within the next six months. With the first four decision makers that I spoke with, I simply recited the "assistant's script" with minor modifications and paused.

One by one, each decision maker responded with a desire to establish an appointment with me. Can you picture this scenario? For almost two years, I had been working hard to see these 30 key decision makers without success and then in one month I have appointments with 25 of them! By the end of Friday afternoon, I sat in my chair unable to move from shock. I could not have been happier.

On that Thursday and Friday, thoughts kept racing through my mind including:

- "What to do next, now that I have *real* appointments?"
- "How am I going to explain everything that is happening to my manager?"
- "How do I interest these high level executives in doing business with me?"

One week before, I was going home in despair. Now, I was going home for the weekend in triumph. I started finding answers very quickly and transitioned to the next step quite nicely. Hey, a man can only live on Hamburger Helper for so long.

Soon after I began to have appointments with my "Top 30," my ranking among the company's nationwide sales force went from being very low to number one for six consecutive months. As you may guess, people at my company began asking questions soon after the weekly sales reports showed much larger-than-average sales in my name. Understanding how successful the first 30 notes had been, I began duplicating the original efforts week after week.

"What are you doing to achieve these high numbers, Mike?" asked Gary, my sales manager. Gary had been extra patient and helpful with me since I started working for the company so I told him the complete introductory note story during a quiet lunch. Soon, the two owners of the company and Gary asked me to travel to the branch offices of the company and teach other salespeople what I am about to share with you.

Many people think preparing an introductory note to high-level key decision makers is easy. Proceed deliberately, because successful implementation of my introductory note comes from paying close attention to the details. Personalized notes have a freshness and personal warmth. The type of card, its color, the fact that there is no return address on the envelope, all meant it often got to the decision maker's desk unopened. I had found a unique approach to establishing a relationship before a face-to-face appointment. The process is the same regardless of whether you are looking for new employment or new business.

You Have to Have a Stable Full of Horses Before You Can Ride...

The first step in your introductory note program is to have a complete list of the companies you wish to work with at the very beginning. The important information to obtain for each record is the company name, address and phone number – that is it!

When you are trying to define your target markets, profile your present customers to determine the people most profitable for you to contact. Over the period of several days, think of all groups of customers and contacts that can benefit from what you have to offer.

For example, you provide a Web site design service and enjoy working with manufacturing and service businesses within a 50-mile radius of your office and would like to include them in your list of companies to work with. Let us carry the example further and suppose you want to specialize in machine tool manufacturing and advertising agencies within your metropolitan area to also include in your list.

Now we need to assemble a list of your favorite prospects that fit your criteria. I prefer the use of directories. Examples of list sources include:

- Chamber of Commerce directories
- Specialized industry/trade directories
- Compiled lists from list brokers
- Employment classified ads

- Business and industrial directories
- Business section of your phone book
- Business Journal lists

My preference is to obtain compiled lists from list directory brokers and trade directories of specialized industries. I cross review these lists with Dun & Bradstreet companies rated CC2 or higher and the business section of my phone book. After all this work, I have a high quality list with which to start. Again, once you determine that a list of companies is attractive for your prospecting efforts, all the information you need is the company name, address and phone number.

Once you have a complete list of your prospects, you are ready to go to the next step, which is organizing your contact records and database. If the ultimate number of prospects you wish to work with is under 50, a well-organized, paper-based system will work just fine. When your prospect numbers rise above 50, however, it is wise to enlist the help of a professional contact software program.

Three of the more popular contact programs are:

- Symantec - Act! (480-368-3700)
- Front Range Incorporated (formerly Gold Mine Corp.) (800-776-7889)
- Maximizer Software (604-601-8000)

All three programs are winners. Your personal preference should be the deciding factor. If you plan to be a heavy-duty FAX user, consider WinFAX Pro by Symantec (same company as Act!) because this program has templates that allow you to include much of your own comments in each record. If you plan to use a paper-based system, the information for each record will be the same as those using contact software.

There are countless variations to building a contact database, but here are some notable fields to include in every record:

- Decision maker's name and assistant's name(s)
- Company name, address ... phone and fax numbers
- Web and e-mail addresses
- Comments (record the person to whom you speak with, date, time of day and what you discussed on **each** conversation you have with someone at the prospect's company).

The two most underrated fields in a contact record are the "Web address" and the "comments" fields. Before initial contact with a decision maker on my list, I want to view their company's Web site thoroughly and learn everything possible about this company. Reviewing a company Web site beforehand enables me to converse intelligently with my prospect. Recording details of every conversation such as date, time, and other people I speak with during this call in the "comments" field is a **necessity**. Months after a conversation, details in your "comments" field will provide help in cementing a relationship with this prospect. You can recall you spoke with so and so, about such and such, at a certain time, which illustrates your organizational abilities and develops excellent rapport. Good notes in my prospect record have given me an edge many times. Now we are ready to systematically update each record you have with fresh information to use in your introductory note.

Your next step is to phone each entry on your target list to update the "record" with the decision maker's name and title that matches your market. In addition, do your best to obtain other helpful information, such as the company Web site and the decision maker's e-mail address. Gather as much information as you can without being bothersome to the person on the other end of the phone.

For example, you have a list of all the machine tool manufacturers in your metropolitan area and want to meet the Vice President of Operations over the phone or on a face-to-face appointment. You systematically phone each machine tool manufacturer on your initial list and ask the person answering the phone for the name of the Vice President of Operations, confirm the company's address (because lists are often surprisingly outdated), and obtain the decision maker's e-mail address and the company Web site. Then thank the answering party for their help. The initial person answering the telephone typically transfers your call to the assistant closest to the decision maker you are trying to reach, who gives you all this information.

One minute ... that is it! Keep in mind that every call is an information opportunity. Here is my script for a typical conversation:

> "Hi, this is Michael McCann with The Business Cafe™. I briefly need your help. I want to send an introductory note to the Vice President of Operations at Xenia Machine Tool & Dye but I do not know to whom to address the note. Can you help me please?"

Then wait for a response.

Often, the person to whom you are speaking will be glad to give you the information because you have said this will be a brief call and you need their help. This is a reminder to always ask for the company's Web address and any specific personal e-mail address for later use. Many decision makers are impressed when they discover you have studied their company prior to talking with them.

When an assistant gives you the name of your probable decision maker, immediately recite the address you have for this business and ask if this is correct. You will be amazed how often the address for the decision maker you have is different from your printed list.

DO NOT ask to speak with the decision maker. What you want to do is "separate yourself from your competition" by sending a low key, non-threatening **written** introductory note to the person who can say "yes" or "no" to you. Have patience and later you will get the ear you wish to hear your message.

You can realistically update 25 company records with all the information you need in one hour. Once you make personal contact with a rented contact list, you **own** the records. Only update the number of records you intend to use for three weeks at one time to maintain the freshness of the information. Having information that is current within one month is critical to the success of the introductory note. Following these two preliminary steps of assembling a prospect list and using the telephone to update information, you will be ready to compose your "connecting" introductory note.

The next step is to prepare a small and personalized note, centered on the thoughts of your recipient, to introduce you as a person. The key here is to introduce you as a person, not your product or service. People buy from people. People want to trust those they buy from, so it is imperative to first establish a relationship of trust with the person who can sign for payment of what you have to offer.

When you are contacting prospects by mail, remember that decision makers will respond well to these four points:

1. Write as you talk. Use plain, ordinary English, Spanish, whatever your language ... exactly the kind you use in everyday conversation.

2. Write from the other person's point-of-view. Tell your recipient what is in it for them ... the same you do in face-to-face presentations.

3. Be explicit. Remember you will not be there to answer questions.

4. Put in a firm "hook." If you are trying to set an appointment, say so. Leave no doubts as to the precise response you want.

If you are up to your eyebrows in work now, start with 30 notes per week. If you are up to your knees in work now, start with 75 notes per week. Important issue here is for you to comfortably deal with **each** recipient as though they are the **only** note you mailed that week. We are going to cover follow up soon.

My first introductory notes were on stationery from a Hallmark store in 1983, using plain blue paper with Hallmark envelopes bearing the Hallmark watermark on the envelope flap. Each week, I mailed 30 "personal" notes to my target market. Today, names and addresses are input into my contact base from which a direct imprint of note and envelope are made.

On the envelope, you want to convey a personal effect so only put the person's name, company name and address with no return address. The envelope needs to have a **matching** First-class stamp that is hand-affixed such as the one below.

Contact Name
Company
Address
City, State Zipcode

The individual who will be following up on the note signs the note. In the opening paragraph, mention some small point that "anchors" the prospect with you such as:

- "Every day I pass your office and notice the beautiful granite company sign ..."

- "I saw your name in the Business Journal and am impressed with your views ..."

- "Your fireplace logs were a big help in heating my home this winter." (I actually used this opening with the President of a fireplace manufacturing company. He became one of my biggest customers).

Your first paragraph must grab your prospect by the eyelashes – and hold on! The first few lines of your note will make or break the success of the note itself. Why? Because almost everyone's eyes start reading there. You want to make sure those eyes continue.

In-between the opening and the close of the note, you will be emphasizing your benefits, adding features and reinforcing credibility, if the need arises. This can mean such things as benefits/features, customer testimonials, descriptions with *specific* examples and always to you, you, and you. Before closing, go back to your big benefit and major selling points once again, and tie in with your original lead, space permitting. The final paragraph includes wording like, "I will call you later in the week to schedule a brief meeting to discuss two ideas that I believe you will be interested in using at (company name)."

If you think direct response copywriters are absent minded just because many, if not most, use letters that carry a "P.S.", think again. It is just another rule or technique that always seems to work. People do *read* the "P.S." Even when the first few lines of the letter cannot hold the reader's attention, the "P.S." offers another chance. This makes it a good place to repeat an important selling point or to pop in a new or different benefit. Sometimes you can use a "P.P.S." I cannot prove to you that it always works but, like chicken soup – it cannot hurt.

Let us look at an example of the introductory note mailed to a machine tool manufacturer in your market centered on the thoughts of the Vice President of Operations to introduce you as a person.

(Date)

Mr./Ms. _____, Vice President
Xenia Tool Die Manufacturing
1112 Reina Drive
Omaha, NE 32023

Dear (Vice President's name):

In speaking with Vice Presidents of other manufacturing tool companies on a regular basis, I understand you are concerned with lost production from broken tools. I am successfully helping four tool and dye companies in the Midwest cut their downtime by 34 percent using specially lubricated equipment from our Michigan plant.

I have two ideas for Xenia Tool & Dye Manufacturing that I want to briefly pose to you when I call later this week. If you are like other Vice Presidents of tool companies that I speak with consistently, I can help you minimize your downtime and can show you how.

In the meantime, please feel free to:

- call me at 614-555-5555; fax 614-555-5555
- e-mail me at Mike@BusinessCafeOnline.com
- visit my Web site at http://www.BusinessCafeOnline.com.

Michael McCann

P.S. Ask me about our special rates for ASTA members.

The notes were originally prepared every Friday and mailed the following Monday morning (holiday mailings were at other times). Many recipients would have the note on their desk between Tuesday morning and Thursday morning. A follow-up call would be made on Thursday afternoon or Friday morning.

If the prospect is out of town when I follow up, which is not uncommon for my prospects, I leave a message. If the prospect is nearby when I am talking to the assistant, I call again without leaving a message, until the decision maker comes to the phone. Should the prospect call when I am unavailable, our receptionist or office manager quickly accesses their name on my contact base and asks if the person has received the personal note from me. If the recipient received the note, Sherry or Pam in our office tells the prospect that I am interested in a brief meeting to discuss two ideas and asks if there is a convenient time for me to call again.

Often the recipients of my "Hallmark" notes are surprised and impressed that my note has "dodged" their staffs' scrutiny. The reactions to the "little blue note" are varied. A surprising number of men told me their staff was not sure if my note was from their mother, wife, woman friend, son or daughter so their staff did not open to "screen." A sizable number of women executives had similar comments.

The size of the envelope, the intimate look and the lack of a return address prompt many staff members to leave my note alone ... making it successful in reaching my prospect. Thankfully, many businesspeople have had a sense of humor over the years. When I succeed in getting "past their staff" while others have failed, many management prospects want to meet me, if for no other reason than to see who this is that succeeded in reaching them directly!

The note should be laser printed on 8½" x 11" high-quality paper on a designated section of each page and then razor cut to fit into a personalized A-2 or A-6 envelope with a double fold. Small, personal-sized envelopes are critical to the success of this program. The staff at the prospect's business needs to believe that your note is personal to the decision maker and let the envelope pass through unopened. I use A-2 size envelopes from Hallmark with the Hallmark seal embossed on the flap of the envelope. You can buy nice, small envelopes and hand emboss a custom seal on each one.

Each envelope is printed with only the addressee's information. I never print a return address because the record is so fresh that there should be no problem in deliverability. Also, a return address on the envelope can signal the person opening the mail that this note is unsolicited and could be thrown away before being opened. Remember, in order to add to that personal look, hand stamp each envelope with a matching First-class stamp. Never use a postal indicia or bulk rate stamp. Keep in mind that you are trying to obtain new business, so this extra effort is well worth the time and investment.

For the decision makers in my immediate vicinity, I mail the weekly notes on Monday morning. For decision makers outside my area and within the United States, I mail the notes the Saturday morning prior to the week I will be calling. The plan here is for the note to reach the decision maker on Tuesday or Wednesday. Tuesdays and Wednesdays are the slowest business mail days of the week and decision makers will likely have just finished the weekly deluge from the meetings and mail on Monday.

Up to this moment, the notes you mail "soften the beachhead". Now you phone each recipient over the next two weeks to introduce yourself, if they have not called you first. I systematically call half my mailed notes on Thursday afternoon and the second half on Friday morning. You need to keep in mind "industry quirks" on when or when not to call during the week. For example, in the manufacturing tool illustration, Mondays and Fridays are the worst days of the week for calling ... just a quirk in the tool industry. As you become familiar with your target industries, you will easily be able to call at the most opportune times.

Use the "Rule of 3"

Assume you mail a note on Monday, August 4, 2003, and call the decision maker for the first time on Thursday, August 7, and you do not make the connection. The best thing to do is find out from an assistant the best time to try again.

If it is possible to leave a message on the decision maker's voice mail – DO SO! Remember, when you leave a message on voice mail, indicate **a specific time (in their time** zone) you will try for the second time. On the following Tuesday, August 12, try to connect in the early afternoon for the second time. If you find a repeat scenario to August 7, then wait until the following Monday, August 18, to try the third and last time. If the decision maker is "not available" for any one of these attempts, there is not sufficient interest to sustain a business relationship at this time and it is best to put this record aside for the moment.

A typical follow-up call will go something like this:

Assistant: "Hello, this is Carolyn, may I help you?"
You: "Hi, Carolyn. My name is Michael McCann with The Business Cafe™. I want to add a brief voice to the small note that I just mailed to Don King. Is he available now?"

Quite often, this approach works very well in connecting calls. Remember that the assistant has your future in their hands so you have to show this person the same respect and attention you extend to the key decision maker. Once you are speaking with the decision maker, a typical conversation starts like this:

Decision Maker: "Hi, this is Don King."
You: "Hello, Mr. King. My name is Michael McCann with The Business Cafe™. I just want to add a brief voice to the note that I mailed to your attention this week. We have been working with (Don's industry) for the past (number of) years. I have two ideas to help you increase your competitive edge in the industry. Can we meet briefly next Tuesday morning or Wednesday afternoon?"

In this brief interaction, you are reinforcing the words from the note you just mailed to the decision maker's attention. The decision maker should also be prepared for this conversation from reading the personal-size note you just mailed within the last three days. When the key decision maker is not available on the first follow-up call, leave your name, company name and thank the assistant for their time. Mention you will be calling again on Monday, Tuesday or Wednesday the following week at a specific time. If the assistant tells you none of these times is going to work, ask for a suggestion on when to call back.

You can see that your second round of calls will be made while you are waiting for your most recent mailing to be delivered. You will soon be following up five days a week as a regular activity. After you get the gist of this system, you will have the confidence to really let your personality show and enjoy making follow-up calls ... accepting the challenge of reaching the person who can say "YES."

What to Say When the Decision Maker Calls You First

From my experiences, seven percent of the notes you mail will elicit a call from the decision maker's office prior to your connecting on your initiated call. Sometimes, this is a "test" by the decision maker to see what will happen if you are challenged unexpectedly. Other times, the decision maker will call or ask an assistant to call and convey:

- "The decision maker will be out of town when you have indicated you will be calling." A call from an assistant gives you the opportunity to build rapport with this person before you speak with the decision maker and find out the best time to call.

- "Your service does not apply to this person but your note is being forwarded to the appropriate person." Usually you are told to whom the note is being forwarded or, if not told, then ask for that person's name. This is a great referral! Wait three business days and call the referral.

- Your service just does not relate to this decision maker's company at all, or the decision maker for this company is in a distant headquarters and the recipient does not want you to waste any more time or money. This information is very helpful because you now know who is **not** your prospect at the moment.

Your ability to sound confident, relaxed and sincere to the person calling you, as though this activity is perfectly normal, is a **key to your success**. After a few weeks of mailing introductory notes, this activity **will be** normal.

The recipient's assistant calls you ... adjust your timing...

Caller: "Hello, Michael. This is Sara from Xenia. Rosalyn Davidson received your note yesterday. She wanted me to let you know she will be out of town until next Tuesday. You indicated you are calling later this week. Can you please call next Tuesday?"

Responder: "Thank you for calling and keeping me informed, Sara. I will be very busy Tuesday, but I will make sure to call Ms. Davidson during a break. Which two-hour period is the best to call next Tuesday?"

The decision maker is someone else ... great because there is an implied referral...

Caller: "Hello, Michael. This is Sara from Xenia. You sent a nice blue note to Rosalyn Davidson and she asked me to give you a call. Rosalyn is not the person who signs off on manufacturing tool dyes for Xenia, but she has forwarded your note to Jack Brown. Ms. Davidson suggested that you call Jack in a few days. You can reach Jack at 555-5555."

Responder: "Sara, thank you and Ms. Davidson for calling and giving me the correct information. When is usually the best day and time to call Mr. Brown?"

This decision maker in a distant city... great way for you to build rapport...

Caller: "Hello, Michael. This is Sara from Xenia. Ms Davidson received your note today and appreciated your thinking of our company. All our machine tool dye agreements are handled in Minneapolis (you are 2,000 miles from Minneapolis). Ms Davidson has no authority in that department."

Responder: "Thank you and Ms. Davidson for your help. Who is the proper person in the Minneapolis headquarters? (wait for answer) Do you have the address and phone number available? I want to introduce myself to (the Minneapolis decision maker) with a brief note in a professional manner."

Adjust the numbers you mail and keep great records. Soon you will have trouble finding the time to make presentations to someone unless they are ready to "come on board."

Helpful Hints

- **List** – Develop your target market list initially with only company name, address and phone number.

- **Phone** – Contact each company to acquire the decision maker's name that corresponds with the highest-level decision maker that can make a decision to say "yes" to your proposal.

- **Contact database** – Be sure to always have the freshest data on the:

  - decision maker's name (or multiple decision maker's names)
  - confirmed, updated address
  - decision maker's e-mail address and their company Web address
  - detailed comments about each conversation you have with ANYONE at the prospect's company

Building the "connecting" introductory note –

Paper

Size:	8 ½" x 11"
Color:	light blue or bright white
Fabric:	25% cotton
Margins:	5" wide x 9" long
Local printer:	"razor cut" the paper from your template
Double-fold:	note into personal-size envelope

Envelope

Personal-size envelope matching your paper selection, such as an A-2 or A-6 size

DO NOT USE #10 ENVELOPES

Addressee information typed or neatly printed on envelope

No return address (A return address signals unsolicited mail)

No enclosed business card

Postage

> First-class, business-like postage stamps blending with the color of the envelope

Timing

> For decision makers in your city, date and mail the notes Monday morning so they should be received on Tuesday or Wednesday that week.
>
> For out-of-town recipients, date and mail notes Saturday morning the week before you call. Postal research studies (ok, let us give the post office the benefit of doubt for accuracy) consistently show that Tuesdays and Wednesdays are the slowest business mail days ... this is a perfect time for your note to show up on the decision maker's desk.
>
> Follow up with the decision maker within three business days of expected receipt of the note, make your appointment and watch your business grow.

Chapter 15

"Breaking the Ice" with Postcards

Postcards are a simple way to communicate with customers on an ongoing basis, but they are not an automatic replacement for solo mailings. The challenge to every businessperson is to constantly look for ways to be unique AND professional, so you will stand out with your audience. I want to show how postcards achieve this goal.

Here are 21 opportunities where postcards can work for your message:

1. **Cost:** Postcards are less expensive to produce than other direct mail formats.

2. **First-Class Delivery:** Sending a postcard First-class is less than two-thirds of the cost of a letter.

3. **Fast Read:** Postcards take seconds to read, increasing the chance they will get read.

4. **Referrals:** Use a double postcard to generate customer referrals (more expensive than standard postcards). A double postcard is two postcards folded together ... one acting as a card for the recipient to fill in and mail back.

5. **Reminders:** Use a postcard to remind customers "there's still time" to shop your sale, order from your latest catalog, RSVP – you name it!

6. **Thank You:** Send a postcard to thank a customer for stopping by, placing an order, waiting for a back order or allowing you to help with his or her holiday gift giving needs.

7. **Sale Preview:** Mail postcards to your best customers to give them the first crack at sales prices and other exclusive offerings.

8. **Private Sale:** Notify your best customers of a private sale.

9. **Deadline Extension:** Use a postcard to extend a deadline for ordering, registering or taking advantage of a limited time special offer.

10. **Invitation:** Use a postcard for a high impact, easy to read invitation that is also easy to retain and refer to.

11. **Pre-Show Mailing:** Send postcards to customers inviting them to visit your booth at an upcoming trade show.

12. **Post-Show Mailing:** Send postcards to customers after a show to thank them for stopping by your booth.

13. **Web site Address:** Launching a Web site? Send the address to customers on peel-off stickers affixed to postcards.

14. **Change in Plans:** Mail postcards to let customers know of a change of address, date change, name change, phone and/or fax number change.

15. **OOPS!** Mistakes happen. Simple and fast to produce, postcards are perfect for saying, "We goofed!" and providing correct information.

16. **Happy Birthday:** Send a postcard in honor of your customer's birthday.

17. **Happy Anniversary:** Acknowledge a customer's loyalty with a postcard on the anniversary of his first purchase.

18. **Upgrade & Cross-Sell:** Send a postcard to your customer who just made a purchase to make a special upgrade or cross-sell offer.

19. **Your Opinions Matter:** Send a double postcard survey (more expensive than standard postcards). A double postcard is two postcards folded together ... one acting as a card for the recipient to fill out and mail back.

20. **Slow Sales:** Sales unexpectedly slow? Send a special offer postcard inviting customers to (1) find your catalog, place an

order now and save, or; (2) stop by your business within the next two weeks and save, or; (3) e-mail, call or fax an order by a specific deadline and save.

21. **Personal Appeal:** Send hand-signed "picture postcards" for high impact and personal appeal. Link the picture and message. For example, send a cable car postcard as an invitation to a trade show in San Francisco or use a picture postcard from Switzerland to introduce a new product made in Geneva. (For added impact, you can even pay to have the postcard mailed from overseas).

When I was trying to introduce myself to my target market in a telephone headset business, I did not have the mammoth budget of AT&T ... the staff of GM or the ad agency of Southwest Airlines. Typically, professional letters cost between $0.50 to $4.50 apiece to distribute. Ouch! Too rich for my blood. I had to be professional on a peanut butter budget and ice tea creativity!

A mailing list broker from whom I had been purchasing lists over the past few years always sent me a postcard to just keep in touch. I thought this was a nice approach ... if I could *improve the quality* of the postcard that he mailed to me.

Through research on the Internet, I found several postcard manufacturers and contacted each one. The postcard printer that stood out from the rest was U.S. Press in Valdosta, Georgia (see *Appendix*). The economic order quantity of postcards that made sense for an initial order was 5,000. That is a lot of cards for testing an idea, but I reasoned I could use them over a 1-2 year period.

What did I put on these postcards? The customer service personnel at U.S. Press were very helpful in recommending which business stock photos were their most popular ones and why. One afternoon, a funny idea came to mind: "Why do I have to show a product of mine on this postcard?   Why not just show an interesting photo and describe my product on the back of the card?"

Different people in customer service at U.S. Press and I took at least one hour discussing numerous professional stock photos available from the printer that would be interesting to recipients that I could use on my postcard. We finally agreed on a beautiful picture of a dolphin with its head above the teal ocean water. Now I know you must be asking yourself, "What does a dolphin have to do with selling telephone headsets (the business I owned at the time)?" Nothing!

Here is an example of the postcard that was used:

TELEPHONE HEADSETS

Customer service personnel at U.S. Press and I wordsmithed the copy covering telephone headsets on the back of the card quickly. The hard part had been deciding the 4 color visual on the front. I took a deep breath and ordered 5,000 cards.

When two heavy boxes with 5,000 postcards arrived, the first 250 cards went to my most die-hard customers. I wanted to confirm what I thought should happen with people who knew me first, before I sent cards to prospects that did not know me. Patiently I waited for any calls and initiated calls to some of these recipients over the next two weeks. The response in both directions was great!

Typical responses from these initial recipients who received the postcard were:

- "I put your dolphin postcard on my bulletin board this winter and it is gone now. Can you send 5 more postcards for people in the office to put up on their bulletin boards?" (Answer: Yes!)

- "I was going to call you about our headset needs soon, but your colorful postcard prompted me to call you today." (You can see me smiling...).

Responses from my best customers were so good the first

two weeks that I realized this program was a winner! Over the next six months, I exhausted the initial 5,000 postcards and had to reorder.

Calls kept coming in from prospects and customers, as well as their staffs, who vocally wondered what a dolphin had to do with telephone headsets. Nothing, except to get them to call me ... opening the door to my presentation on the phone. (By the way, I love dolphins and I love the water ... the dolphin postcard is still on my bulletin board).

Here is what the math looked like on my postcard program:

5,000 postcards	$ 525.00 (after setup, freight free with prepayment)
labels	150.00
postage ($0.23 ea.)	1,150.00
Total	$1,825.00 (plus "soft" costs like your time, etc.)

For minimal effort and great retention by prospects and customers, my out-of-pocket costs came to $0.365 each (plus administrative time, etc.). For the results, you cannot beat the price.

Helpful Hints

* **"The Look"** – All postcards do not have to look the same. Oversized postcards may cost more to produce and mail, but they also stand out in the mail. Splurge on paper; postcards are visual and tactile.

* **Stamps** – Hand-affixed, First-class (postcard stamps) look more personal and interesting than a printed indicia or metered postage.

* **Economy of Scale** – Create a series of postcards and print them all at once to save money.

* **Encourage Interactivity** – Get readers involved with peel-off stickers, tipped-on magnets, scratch-and-sniff, etc.

* **Keep Your Eyes Open** – Check your mail and talk to printers for additional postcard ideas that do not cost a fortune.

Chapter 16

The "One-Two" Letter Punch

Secrets to the Successful Two-Step Letter

Want your prospects to qualify themselves? That is right! Implementing this two-step letter program will virtually keep qualified leads coming to you. No need to phone or see your prospects face-to-face before implementing this program. Mail as many as you wish for the returns you can comfortably handle.

You need to plan at least a month in advance to mail one to two prospecting letters to a quantity of prospects that you can personally handle. In addition, you will be mailing three professionally produced collateral pieces about your business to each respondent. This whole process probably sounds expensive to you and you are probably asking what "the numbers" look like. Here is an example:

Step 1: Mail 1,000 letters with a 4" x 6" Business Reply Card to your prime prospects. You get a Business Reply Card returned from 8 percent to 12 percent of these recipients (say, 100 responses =10 percent).

Step 2: Mail a copy, on yellow paper, of a similar letter along with an identical Business Reply Card to the first letter as in Step 1, to the 900 prospects that did not respond. You are likely to soon get a Business Reply Card from 24 percent to 35 percent (say, 300 responses =30 percent).

You now have 400 positive responses from prospects with specific information on whom the decision makers are and where to mail your information about your company. For now, put the 600 non-responsive names aside and focus on the 400 who did reply.

Step 3: Create three informative direct mail packages on topics of interest to your 400 prospects. Your collateral needs to give the recipients something of plain value. In addition, each package that you mail to decision makers will contain professionally produced information on your business. The cost of creative and production of these three mail packages can range from a couple of dollars to many dollars per set of three. You are paving the way for the follow-up call, so do not skimp on the quality.

Steps 1 and 2 of the prospect acquisition budget will look something like this:

A. First mail out of 1,000 letters with list input, letter creation, printing on **white** copy paper and company envelopes, Business Response Card on blue paper (assumption made that you have a BRC permit from your post office already), assembling package and First-class postage. These dollar figures include several one time set-up costs:

Approximately $725 for 1,000 letters mailed

B. Second mail out of 900 letters printed on **yellow** copy paper and company envelope, Business Reply Card printing, assembling package and First-class postage:

Approximately $645 for 900 letters mailed

That is a total of $1,370 for locating 400 decision makers at specific addresses by their own company personnel! Where else can you obtain company-qualified leads for only $3.43 each?

Let me continue with more specifics. The first letter you write on white copy paper will look something like this:

July 4, 2003

ABE Company
3258 Buzbee Street
Suarez, MN 44334

Greetings,

Soon your company will begin receiving valuable information for persons involved in making sure your computer network remains up and running at all times. Trouble is, I do not know to whom to address the white papers and other valuable information.

I will appreciate your help today. On the enclosed blue postcard, please include their correct mailing address and to whom this valuable information should be sent. I can assure you the people you refer today will be pleased that you took the time to see that they have the most current information on computer networks.

Thank you …

Michael McCann
Director

The Business Cafe™
(address)
(phone number)

The enclosed Business Reply Card will have the name of the company receiving the letter imprinted in the specified block (blue 4" x 6" size) and will have copy like the following illustration.

The first group of 1,000 letters, with Business Reply Cards, needs to be mailed on a Monday morning. Responses will be coming back for the next two to three weeks. Exactly three weeks after the first mailing, mail the second letter on **yellow** copy paper to those who have not responded yet with similar wording to the first letter.

(Blue paper)

I do not know to whom to address the valuable papers being sent to your company soon. I will appreciate your help today. Please include the name of the appropriate people and their titles on the blanks below and return this postage-paid card today. Please indicate any change of address necessary below. Thank you.

ABE Company
3258 Buzbee Street
Sucony, MN 44334

Name   Title

_____   _____

_____   _____

(Yellow paper)

July 25, 2003

ABE Company
3258 Buzbee Street
Suarez, MN 44334

Greetings,

Three weeks ago, I mailed a letter to your attention asking for your help. Soon your company will begin receiving valuable information for persons involved in making sure your computer network remains up and running at all times. Trouble is, I do not know to whom to address the white papers and other valuable information.

This is my second request for your help. On the enclosed blue postcard, please include their correct mailing address and to whom this valuable information should be sent. I can assure you the people you refer today will be pleased that you took the time to see that they have the most current information on computer networks.

Thank you ...

Michael McCann
Director

The Business Cafe™
(address)
(phone number)

Use the same blue response card in the second mailing as you included in the first letter.

You will receive approximately 30 percent response from the second letter by the end of the second week. Within five weeks of beginning this program, you should have approximately a 40 percent response rate. Not bad for just mailing letters to companies without lifting the phone or leaving the office!

Now that you have approximately 400 blue response cards with decision makers' names in your hands, what is next? Mail three evenly timed information packages to each person with the intention of adding value to their job and communicating your company message at the same time. I mail each of the three packages three weeks apart.

Six Steps To Better Information Packages

Treating an information letter the same way as a direct sell (one-step) letter is a common mistake. Although there are similarities between the two relating to the basic rules of good direct marketing copy, there are some striking differences.

To get the most from your mailings to prospects and customers, use this six-point checklist.

1.   Know what you are offering.

Unless you deal with this question properly, you can destroy your chances for success. You are not just delivering information; you are trying to get qualified prospects to become customers. That means you want prospects to write, call or fax you their questions and thoughts. You have to give them a good reason to go to the effort.

Inexperienced direct marketers often offer "more information." You are asking your prospect to raise their hand and say, "please sell me something," and most people will not help you sell them something. You will lose some measure of qualified response with an information offer.

The best direct mail piece promises some intrinsic value to your prospect, independent of the information you want to convey. Here is an example: I created an inexpensive piece for a computer hardware company designed to help prospects determine the best computer configuration for their needs. The resulting piece had a fundamental, objective measure of value for anyone considering the purchase of a new PC. (And no value for anyone not considering the purchase of a new PC, making it an excellent qualifying mechanism).

The computer company received three benefits: First, any respondent was almost certainly considering buying a new PC. Second, a relationship had been established for further marketing efforts. Third, it became possible to select the parameters on which the prospect would base the purchase decision. (A new products catalog and sales letter mailed with the "objective" planning guide).

2. **Be clear about what you want your prospect to do immediately after reading your letter.**

If you do not know, the prospect will not know either. Figure it out and tell him or her to do it. "Call 1-800-555-1421 right now to receive your ..." If your call-to-action is weak or confused, your response will be weak.

3. **Write in a one-to-one style.**

Use "you, your, you will, you are" often. Use "we, we will, us, our" as little as possible.

This is a personal communication between you and one other person. Avoid making it sound like an ad. The objective is to use personal influence to convince one person at a time. Write to communicate. Save big words, long sentences, and complex concepts for your next job interview (kidding).

4. **Do not tell them what you want them to know.**

Tell prospects only what they need to know to do what you want them to do. You know tons of great things about your company's products and services, and you would probably like to tell everyone. The fact is, nobody cares. People care about items they can use. If the items they can use are buried in the things you want them to know, they will simply throw the whole information package in the trash.

5. **Do not tell your prospects the whole story.**

You want your most qualified prospects to identify themselves. The best way to do this is to raise questions that only your best buyers will find compelling. Then tactfully tell them they can find the answers to these and related questions when they respond (again, telling them only what they need to know).

Example: If you are trying to generate business for a consumer gardening catalog, you can raise these questions in your letter: "There are more than 20 varieties of tomatoes in our new 2004 catalog, and four are brand new this year. See these and more than 700 other varieties of fruits, bulbs, vegetables, and trees when you send for your FREE 2004 (brand name here) catalog."

Notice, there is no formal question. I raised a question in the prospect's mind. More important, the question raised is not important to a non-gardener. Only an avid gardener, a qualified lead, will find this missing information worth requesting.

6. **"Long copy" vs. "short copy" rules do not apply (whatever they are).**

This is lead generation. You are not asking for a buying decision; you want potential prospects to raise their hands and tell you they are interested in your message. If you have taken Point 4 to heart, you are not likely to require a lot of words to do the job. When you have said what you need to say, your letter is long enough.

Your first package can include a booklet summarizing the latest major trade show highlights on computer networking with your input on what these highlights mean for these decision makers. Be sure to include professional collateral on your company in this package.

The second package can contain a booklet outlining trends you see in the computer networking industry and what several companies are doing now to prepare. Again, remember to include professionally produced materials on your company.

The last envelope should include a personalized cover letter from you showing your desire to help the recipient in his/her career with information you have provided. Insert another booklet with helpful information targeted for the recipient and, of course, your company information.

Up to this moment, the envelopes you have mailed "softened the beachhead". Now you need to phone each recipient within three weeks after mailing the third package to introduce yourself (if they have not called you first).

Adjust the numbers you mail and keep great records. Soon you will only have time to make presentations to someone when they are ready to "come on board".

Helpful Hints

- **Planning** – Careful advance long-term planning is critical to the success of your two-step letter program. Allow at least 2 months' advance planning and three months' planning after mailing the first letter for each group of information package recipients.

- **Simplicity** – Keep the letters and Business Reply Cards simple. Your direct mail package should be simple and emphasize professionalism and your desire to help the decision maker improve their business.

- **Complete** – Answer all the questions in your direct mail package that you think you would have if you were receiving the communiqués from an unknown company.

Chapter 17

Spreading Cheer and Building Your Database

Leverage your presence with customers and prospects by sending them periodic communiqués. Professional and unique holiday greetings help build a bond between you and your business acquaintances. What I am about to reveal to you is a powerful and proven method of standing out from your competition. The success or failure of implementing my holiday greetings program lies in the details.

Let us assume you already have a contact database that is "clean" and ready to merge with an effective marketing program to keep in touch with your prospects and customers. Numerous studies indicate you should contact your important businesspeople in intervals from three weeks (time it takes to form/unform habits) to every three months ("about to forget you" stage). A program that works well for me is sending communiqués tied to every major holiday to your customers and prospects ... next best thing to face-to-face meetings.

The beauty of this approach is your ability to execute the "holiday message" program anywhere in the world. Businesspeople in Singapore can tie communiqués to Singapore's holidays. Mexican businesspeople can coordinate their messages with Mexican holidays. American businesspeople can merge with America's major holidays. Let us use the United States holidays as an example that you can relate to with whatever country's holidays you choose.

Taking a look at my planning calendar, I see the major American holidays (**not** including religious holidays such as Christmas) in the year 2003 are:

New Year's Day	January 1	Independence Day	July 4
Valentine's Day	February 14	Labor Day	September 1
St. Patrick's Day	March 17	Halloween	October 31
Memorial Day	May 30	Thanksgiving	November 27

Your name will be in front of customers and prospects at least eight times in 2003, following the dates above. The fact there is an uneven spread of one to two months between each of these holidays is fine. There are 52 weeks in the year, divided by eight messages, equaling contact an average of every 6.5 weeks.

Picture what your customers and prospects will think when you present them with a *New Year for New Business* card or *Thanksgiving* story in a seasonal envelope. When I receive a well thought out holiday message from a business acquaintance, I think this person is unique and professional. A simple message on a major holiday indicates you have more depth and more to offer than just your company's products and services.

This is the logistics of sending a holiday message to my contact database:

Step 1: Purchase materials and develop your message for each holiday at least four weeks in advance of the holiday.

Step 2: Print materials or write personal messages three to four weeks in advance of the holiday.

Step 3: Personally deliver as many as possible, or mail the greetings two weeks before the holiday.

For my Thanksgiving communiqué, I researched the origins of this holiday and laser-printed the summary story on one parchment looking 8 ½" x 11" sheet. My name, company name and phone number were in small print at the bottom of the page. The story was then inserted in a dark red 9" x 12" envelope with the recipients' name typed on a holiday label.

Two weeks before Thanksgiving, I hand delivered as many of my "stories" as possible. Organizing the recipients by zip code, I delivered 30-plus per day. This delivery episode turned into an exhausting and invigorating exercise. The exhaustive angle does not need explanation. The invigorating side came from seeing customers, prospects and staffs in their offices. I made the extra step to come to the other person's office for no reason than to show a "human" touch at a holiday period.

Many recipients did not know what to say when a businessperson came to their office without asking for anything in return. Office staff displayed expressions of relief. Customers and prospects out of town received their packages about two weeks before Thanksgiving and were equally surprised that there were no strings attached.

They were wrong! There were strings attached to sending my Thanksgiving story. I need to concentrate my time and investments on only my strongest customers and prospects. By visiting many customers' and prospects' offices and calling the "out of towners" after they received their Thanksgiving stories, I systematically built my contact database to concentrate on only the most promising after each conversation.

Look at each holiday greeting as a "contact database cleanser." On my way to being a good businessperson, I want to spread the holiday joy with my best prospects and customers. During each 6.5-week period in our example here, I may add 20 to 50-plus prospects and delete half this number through discovering half of my contact database is not worth my efforts for these specialized communiqués. Also, it is a great way to keep in touch with your customers.

You cannot ask for a better deal than this. Here is to your happy holidays and increasingly prosperous business.

Helpful Hints

- **Participants** – Decide whom your best prospects and customers are and include these people in an initial six-month segment of receiving your communiqués. Re-evaluate your contact list at least every six months.

- **Design** – Plan and begin to acquire materials for each holiday communiqué that will reflect professionalism and uniqueness to you.

- **Delivery** – Hand deliver as many communiqués as possible and mail the remainder First-class mail. Do not ask to speak to the decision maker on personal visits, just deliver the holiday greeting to the decision maker's office staff and briefly exchange small talk to build rapport for later.

Chapter 18

Your Own FACT Page

Want a simple and professional handout that gives your complete business story on one two-sided page? For years, I was asked for a "bio" or description of what I do to give to important decision makers. All of us have heard that voice inside saying, "Ok, I'll prepare my personal bio tomorrow."

Tomorrow is now. Take this journey with me to see how you can have your own FACT page. This all-inclusive, two-sided glossy piece of paper will take several hours to professionally prepare. Once you are finished, though, you will wonder why you waited so long to have this uncomplicated description of yourself to give to others.

The goal of the FACT page you are creating is to have information at your fingertips for times:

- When you are running out of the office and you just finished speaking with an important decision maker on the phone who wants to see your "bio" NOW.

- When you are at decision maker's place of business and an important person asks you to leave information about you and your company.

- When you are unsure about the "please send me a brochure" request you just received. Send your FACT page instead and follow up within a week.

The example shown in Figure 18.1 is a newsletter template, directly processed in Microsoft *Word*. For best results, I prepare a draft of my complete FACT page in *Word*. I then take my two laser-printed pages to a professional printer, where double-sided copies on glossy paper are printed for the finishing touches.

Professionally produce a photograph of yourself on four-color photo stickers to incorporate on your FACT page. By utilizing four-color photo stickers attached to your glossy black-and-white FACT page, the entire piece holds the illusion of being an expensive four-color personal presentation.

Once you have your professional document and color photo copied, you can print professional black and white 8 ½" x 11" copies at establishments that produce high-resolution copies. Expect to pay between $0.15 to $0.20 per two-sided page and attach your sticky color photo in the appropriate box.

Four-color (your photo in color) FACT pages are best for important presentations. You can distribute black and white copies in all other situations.

Debating whether to design your FACT page in four-color or black and white? Color sells! Now all you need to add are quality appointments.

Figure 18.1 – Page 1 (FACT Page template)

Your Name	
Your most profitable product/service at your company <u>or</u> your "special offer" that you want to get premium exposure (you can change this section later).	**Your Photo** **from 5x7 or 4x6** **color photo** **Your name** **Your** biography, including business background, interests, education... to the bottom of this page.

Figure 18.1 – Page 2 (FACT Page template)

What Satisfied clients are saying? e.g.	Description of other products/services you provide...
"Your product helped our company increase our sales by 22% in six months. Thanks!" Jim Thomas, AT&T	
Other Satisfied Customers e.g. *SoftTek, Mexico City, DF* *Schlotzsky's, Austin, Texas*	**How To Contact You** e.g. Michael McCann Managing Director The Business Cafe™ www.BusinessCafeOnline.com

Helpful Hints

- FACT page needs to be one page, two-sided.

- Carry five FACT pages with you every time you leave the office for unexpected requests.

- Keep your FACT page up-to-date. Duplicate only enough copies at one time for no longer than three-month usage.

- Use your FACT page to "multiply" your presence.

Chapter 19

Business Cards and Name Badges

Question. What is? ...

- 2" x 3 1/2";
- works overtime with no complaints for very low cost; and,
- never calls in sick?

Answer: your business cards.

When I have something as small as a business card working this hard for me 24 hours per day, 7 days per week, I sit up and pay attention! Let me share some ideas that have worked well for me in recent years.

First impressions about your professionalism are often formed from perceptions about your business card. Your "tiny billboard" is easily distributed and speaks volumes about you so that care in design and printing is imperative. When working on my most recent business card design, I consumed more ice tea in brainstorming sessions than usual. Thinking about the right logo, right colors, right placement of information and the right wording took more than just a few brainstorming sessions.

The logo on your business card projects your image and perceived value in the social and business hierarchy. For example, the simple logo design Lucent Technologies has with a simple circular pattern in red connotes a direction of vitality and strength to the telecommunications industry. My logo is a professionally drawn caricature of me holding a microphone to convey professionalism in communication. Listening to many businesspeople over the last 25 years, a simple design, executed in an eloquent fashion, wins the most votes for acceptance.

Colors you use on your business card also communicate a powerful message. For example:

- *Red* points to aggression, passion, strength and vitality.
- *Blue* connotes authority, dignity, security and implies fiscal responsibility and security.
- *Gray* portrays a somber, authority, practical, "corporate" tone.
- *Black* illustrates a serious, distinctive, bold and classic tone.

Placement of information on your 2" x 3 1/2" billboard and the right wording sends silent signals to recipients. Beyond the usual information such as name, company, address and phone number are personal choices that illustrate to the world your organizational abilities and what you consider important to convey. For example, do you include?

- your fax number (shows you do not want ANY barriers to communication or you do not want to write down this information every time someone asks for your fax number),

- your Web site address (this is a great idea to include),

- your company slogan (my slogan, "Building Your Business ... one person at a time," elicits many positive comments and gives me a chance to start conversation), and,

- your title.

Now, you have your business cards designed and printed (using high-quality paper) in the image in which you want to be perceived. Let us see how we can effectively utilize your "billboard".

Take your business cards everywhere! Jogging, networking events (ok, this is obvious), lunch with friends on the weekend ... everywhere. Why? You never know when you will encounter the contact that will change your life. When you leave home, always bring your business cards. I include about 10 cards in the opposite side of my small fold over wallet holding other important documents (driver's license, phone card, credit card and calendar card). These 2 1/2" x 4" wallets are available at major office supply stores in a variety of textures and colors (I like brown or black leather). When you "chance upon" someone who can mean a positive impact on your life, you are always capable of presenting your business card.

In addition to having your own business card ready to give, consider someone you meet, and want to meet again, who is not carrying **his or her** business cards. Again, you open **your** wallet, pull out **two** cards: One for the person to keep and the other card for the person to write their information on the back and hand back to you on the spot. People who have been privy to this method remark how impressed they are that I have my business cards ready for giving and receiving (back).

Say you meet someone who asks you for information; you can write the answer in a small space. Guess where you will write the answer? Yes, the back of your business card. One person I know keeps a set of business cards (in addition to conventional cards) that only includes his name, company name and phone number so he can take an extra moment with each contact to "fill-in-the blanks" on the back of the card in person.

When faxing information to businesspeople, place your business card in an area of the fax cover sheet that is non-essential. You may need to use a special paper holder because of the extra thickness of the paper being faxed ... the results in appearance are worth it. Your business card has the look and the information that is hard to personalize on fax cover sheets.

From One Card to Another
Planning Ahead to be Impromptu

Have you ever gone to a business event and wondered how to "circulate" with people totally unknown to you? I am now going to reveal two ways to exchange business cards and meet new businesspeople at your next meeting.

Last fall, I was engaged to speak before a civic group and really wanted every audience member's business card. Trouble was, I needed all the available time to prepare for the presentation onsite. I had brought a nice sauce bowl from my kitchen to put audience business cards in but had no idea how to circulate this dish around the room. A lady at my table graciously said, "Let me help, I will go to each table with the bowl and accumulate everybody's business card." I promptly accepted, without knowing the outcome. Away she went with my sauce bowl and a smile.

About 30 minutes later, just as the program was to begin, my newfound luncheon acquaintance returned to my table with a sauce bowl full of business cards. "How did you motivate everyone to contribute their business card?" I asked. "I just went table to table meeting people and asked everyone to put their card in the bowl for a door prize drawing at the end of the presentation ... everybody gladly obliged," she said. Thankfully, I had brought copies of my audiocassette program for people in the audience to purchase after my presentation. We quickly concluded this would be the door prize. This whole door prize episode was totally unrehearsed and unexpected, but I thought about what happened with this lady and the business cards she had accumulated a few days later.

What my table companion accomplished is open to anyone at a business meeting of strangers. You can bring a nice dish to drop business cards into and walk from table to table-meeting new people and exchanging business cards. You can have a drawing for a prize after the presentation. If you have a drawing or prize of some sort, be sure to mention **all** the details when meeting people. You can simply tell people you want to remember them after the meeting and want to exchange "pleasantries" and a business card. A couple of days after my presentation to this group, I called several people from the audience. How do you think I knew their name and phone number? Their business card. You can attend business meetings with another person from your office. Arrange in advance for one of you to circulate and collect cards. Another option is for both of you to split up and each work half of the group.

At another meeting, I was on the receiving end of another version of the business card idea. While I was patiently sitting at an aisle seat in an auditorium waiting for a keynote to begin, two gentlemen I had never met walked up to me and introduced themselves. The two men worked together and appeared to be professional, so I decided it would be worthwhile to engage in conversation while waiting for the presentation. Each gentleman had collateral describing their businesses that they were distributing to individuals they met in the audience. Both men were quite pleasant in conversation. In this case, I was so impressed with their openness, I offered my business card to each of them. Their business cards were neatly glued in specific spots in their literature, so I felt as if I should at least reciprocate with my card.

I observed these two men after we bid farewell and remained impressed with their style. Both men circulated for at least 30 minutes before the speech and covered many rows, getting similar responses to the one they had received from me. Frankly, I wanted to be doing the same thing they were doing but had not brought enough of my own business cards to go past three or four rows. A few days after I met the two men at the keynote, I received a nice note from the duo. At this point, I sat up and took notice. Unfortunately, I have no reason to develop a business relationship with these two individuals but, if the need did exist, you can bet they would be tops on the list to call.

What did I learn from these two unexpected experiences? In a nutshell, come prepared with your business cards and collateral to meet and greet before the presentation begins. I now have a nice container in my car trunk that is available for circulating around a business meeting to hold other people's business cards. I also keep up-to-date business cards and collateral in the trunk so I can plan in advance to be impromptu.

Put Your Best Name (Badge) Forward

You are looking forward to attending a business mixer with your friends and A-plus prospects. Now, picture this: You make sure your clothes are just right for the occasion and your grooming is the best possible. Upon arrival to the event, the individual at the check-in table asks you to fill in a name badge to identify you quickly to people who wish to know with whom they are speaking. What just went awry? The name badge with your name and company name probably looks just like everyone else's – boring.

The above scenario is repeated over and over throughout the world every day. If you do not like the typical name badge you consistently receive at important business meetings, you need to design your own. Your goal is to have two to three professional name badges that match whatever occasion you attend.

The customized name badge is an idea from a publicist I met while at a conference this summer. The man took me aside in the hotel lobby and did some quick "surgery" to my name badge, producing dramatic improvements. He made a believer out of me. When I wear a professional, customized name badge, people make positive comments. Here are several specific ideas for putting your best name (badge) forward:

Step one: Do not panic. Designing your own professional name badge is easy. The materials you need are readily available from major office supply stores. Keep in mind the result you want to achieve: A professional looking name badge.

Step two: Assemble the materials you need for every name badge you want to create. I have two separate name badges that are ready-to-wear (no, my badges are not "polyester") in order to fit the formality of meeting I am attending. At an office supply, you can find clear plastic badge holders with the low intrusive, clip-style retainer (preserve your fine clothing) as well as white 70# paper. Purchase two clear badge holder sizes: One 3 1/2" x 2 1/4" and the other 4" x 3". In addition to holders and 70# paper, have several of your business cards nearby while at your computer. You will have to experiment with font sizes and word placement on your laser printer to achieve the right placement on the badge. Remember that the long-term results are worth the exercise now.

The following is an example of a 4" x 3" size. You will notice the back shows a magnet.

3 ½" x 2 ¼" size (business card size)

Step three: Start with the smaller name badge. At an office supply store, the 3 1/2" x 2 1/4" size is known as a "business card" size. You need to print and cut this name badge to show professionalism for more intimate and familiar settings. Close to the top line of the 70# paper making up the name badge, laser print your company name in a 14-point type style you like (I like the Times New Roman font). In the middle of the badge laser print, in big letters (at least 18-point), your first name. Just above the bottom, balanced with what you did on the top line, laser print your last name. If you want to add some pizzazz, add your slogan in small print just below your last name. Cut around the print you just made and place in the small name badge for a professional looking introduction.

Step four: Continue with the larger "convention" size badge holder. You need to print this name badge to wear in networking events, conferences and conventions where business is typically of a less intimate nature. You want to create a "live billboard". Start by cutting a piece of 70# paper to fit completely in the 4" x 3" badge holder. Close to the top line of the 70# paper making up the name badge, laser print your company name. In the middle of the badge laser print, in big letters, your first name. Just above the bottom, balanced with what you did on the top line, laser print your last name. You still have plenty of room to laser print what you do and your slogan. My tag line: "Syndicated columnist and trainer" goes across the top in Times Roman 14 point. My slogan: "Building Your Business ... one person at a time" goes just below my tag line in Times Roman 12 point. If you want to add some pizzazz, add your logo to the 70# white easel.

Alternatively, you can have a custom name badge made at a local custom stamp store. Due to the weight of custom badges, you will be prudent to keep the size around 1 1/2" x 3 1/2" or less. Be sure to specify a "clip" on the back to preserve your clothing.

My name badges are kept nearby for quick use. I arrive at event check-in desks with a name badge that I can be proud of in advance. My clothing also likes the fact that no pins pierce the cloth or adhesive pulls threads when the name badge is removed. Making an appearance with a custom name badge speaks highly of your good taste. Participants near you can easily see who you are and get an idea of what you do. The rest is up to you.

As you can see, there are many applications for business cards and name badges. I want to leave you with only one thought: Use professionalism and creativity in your business contacts. Using good taste and creativity can insure your business card, your name badge (and you) will stay forefront in the mind of your target audience.

Helpful Hints

• **Layout and Colors** – Keep business cards and name badges that impress you and decide what it is that you like about these cards and badges ... consider the layouts and colors of your collected cards and badges when producing your own.

• **Professional and Unique** – Design your own card and name badge so it is custom to you. Avoid using templates.

• **Omnipresent** – Take several of your business cards everywhere (and I do mean everywhere) because you never know when a profitable business encounter will occur.

Part V

Connecting on the Phone

Chapter 20

What to Do with That !x%?# Voice Mail

Many people are frustrated and exasperated when they reach answering machines and voice mail. View this technology as another tool to help you develop business or otherwise reach the decision maker. I, too, used to think of digital companions I came in contact with as a crevice in which to exercise futility and leave intelligent information in the hopes that someone listening many years in the future may return my call. One day, I recognized the concept of *controlling* the desired dialogue with my intended recipient and my viewpoint changed regarding digital conversation altogether!

You heard me right ... I said *controlling* the dialogue. Keep in mind that the person who is *calling* is the one who has the greatest chance in *controlling* the conversation. With this concept in mind, try to look at each encounter with a "digital companion" as your chance to move closer to a well-educated conversation eventually with your intended recipient. Let us look at five steps that have helped me maximize my effectiveness and time with "digital companions."

- *Listen to the Entire Message*
  You might hear information that will help you build rapport later. The potential gain is greater than the few seconds you invest.

- *Be Prepared to Leave a Message*
  When you are preparing for this telephone call, prepare to leave a recorded message as well. You will leave a much more favorable impression.

- **Have a Message Objective**
  Leave no doubt as to what should happen as a result of your message. Who is going to do what? Are they to call you (I do not suggest this)? Will you call back (I do suggest this)? What time? (Always speak in terms of their time zone).

- **State Clear Benefits**
  Motivate them to be in a positive frame of mind to accept your next call. You do this by telling them what is in it for them. Constantly think of that famous radio station WIFM ("what is in it for me"). Mention an idea or two that you believe will help them.

- **Leave Essential Information**

  - name (you will be surprised how many messages I receive without names).

  - company name (decision makers want to know your affiliation).

  - phone number (remember area code if you are calling out-of-town).

  - time you called (again, always speak in terms of their time zone).

  - Web site address (if you do not have a web page, get one as soon as possible)!

Let us look at a typical voice mail interaction.

Voice Mail: "Hi, you have reached the voice mail of Lois Lane. I am away from my office. Please leave me a message at the tone and I will return your call as soon as possible."

You: "Lois, this is Michael McCann with The Business Cafe™. I have an idea I would like to provide for you regarding how I have helped other companies in your size range reach key decision makers to increase their revenues and net income over the long-term. Right now, it is 1:25 p.m. Eastern Time on Thursday afternoon. My phone number is (800) 335-8161, and I will be calling you back at 3:45 p.m. Eastern Time today. If you have an opportunity in the meantime, look at my Web site, www.BusinessCafeOnline.com to see several examples of companies I have worked with recently. Looking forward to speaking with you soon."

Let us examine what I just did in this one-minute digital interaction.

- I have given Lois an idea of who I am and what my voice is like so when I call back, my voice and company name will be familiar to her.

- Lois is likely to be curious as to what I have in mind to help her business. After all, who does not want to increase revenues and net income? It will be worth her time to receive my phone call?

- Lois does not have to wonder how long ago I called ... I have told her a fairly exact time and she can look at her watch to figure out how much time has elapsed. Here is a **golden nugget:** Lois, like many voice mail users, is going to be testing me to see if I do call back at 3:45 p.m. Eastern Time as I have said. Pass this time test and you can pass the proverbial "go" in the monopoly game of business.

- If Lois has Internet access and a moment to browse my Web site before 3:45 p.m., she will have an opportunity to become further acquainted with me before I call ... kudos to my web page!

Now, the "ball is still in my court." Shame on me if I made this effort on voice mail and do not call back right at 3:45 p.m. Eastern Time. There are **many** voice mail users who screen calls and will test callers using various means to accept only those that hold the highest credibility based on their "tests."

Stating the right time I **called** is another test many voice mailers use because most voice mail systems "time stamp" each incoming call. Pass this "test" and maybe this recipient will speak with you when you call back.

I prefer to leave incoming times and callback times that are odd numbers because these times are easier for the recipient to remember. When I call back at 3:45 p.m. as expected, I am ready for the "digital companion" again.

I will make three educated tries at making direct connection; each time being ready to leave another message. After the third call, I will slightly alter this script and ask the recipient to call when it is convenient for them. Often, you will receive a "real" call from your digital companion owner after the third call if you have a perceived good match. If no call comes, either the recipient did not think the match was good, or chalk one more up for digital space.

Can You Imagine the Following Voice Mail?

James Dunson, a telecommunications consultant, recently shared this humorous and fictional story with me. I have listened to real voice mail messages that come close to this phone call's absurdity.

Ring, Ring, Ring...

"Thank you for calling Widgetron. If you wish to continue in English, press 1. If you wish to continue in some other language, press 1 and get out a dictionary."

"1"
"If at any time you wish to speak with an operator, hang up and dial "0". For sales information, read our brochure, that is why we print the darn things. If you wish to purchase something, press "1" and then type in your credit card number and expiration date; we will evaluate your credit and send you something appropriate. If you need technical support or to report a problem, press "2".

"2"
"You have reached Widgetron technical support. We are not answering the phone right now, and have absolutely no remorse about it. If you have an onsite service contract on your Widget, that means you need to bring it onto our site for service; we are located on the 3rd island down the Aleutians. Just mention our name to the bush pilot you hire, they all know where we are."

"If you are a nitwit, and probably forgot to plug it in, or have let your 2-year old feed it oatmeal, press, "1" and then hang up and read the instructions and disclaimers."

"If you have any sort of hardware, software, furniture, or other objects not made by Widgetron near the Widget, press "2" to hear an informative recording of why it is not our fault or problem."

"If your Widget, or any other nearby hardware, software, furniture, or other objects, is older than 3 months, press "3" to hear a recorded explanation that says we no longer support it."

"If you are running the Widget under unsupported conditions, we cannot help you. We have tested our Widget with all machines running DOS we could find, and encountered no unexpected difficulties."

"If you are wondering if your Widget is Year 2010 compliant, press "4" for a recording explaining that all Widgets are fully compliant, by the simple expedient of setting their clock back."

"If you are sure that you have covered all the basic troubleshooting information, and wish to declare your problem "Advanced", press "5" and then hang up. One of our Advanced Troubleshooters will arrive and shoot whatever they determine is the trouble."

Time Zones are Important

To share with you a true story illustrating the importance of communicating the correct time zone, the following episode almost became a disaster in my life.

May 1997, I was going to be on a major Detroit, Michigan, radio station via phone from Austin, Texas. When the program's producer left me a voice mail message telling me to be ready at 7:30 a.m., I made a conspicuous note on my calendar so that I would be ready.

Thankfully, I had a lot of work to catch up on, so I arrived at the office about 6:15 a.m. the morning of the interview. About 6:25 a.m., the producer called to ask if I was ready to go on the air in 2-3 minutes. I thought 7:30 a.m. in Detroit, Michigan, was 7:30 a.m. in Austin, Texas, as well. WRONG! Detroit, Michigan, is Eastern Time and Austin, Texas, is Central Time. I since have learned my lesson from this close call (figuratively and literally).

Lesson learned? Now, I ALWAYS confirm the appointments out-of-town, making sure that both of us are talking about the same time zones.

Setting Up Your Own Voice Mail

According to Marcus Grahame, president of a voice mail technology company, GM Productions, "Voice mail should be used as a productive marketing tool. It can maximize your telecommunications investment, give employees a direct line to the latest news, and allow your company to make a good impression and share information of value with the caller."

Good voice mail demands good etiquette.

According to the Voice Messaging Educational Committee, an industry group of leading voice messaging manufacturers and service providers, there are a number of simple suggestions that will help the caller feel comfortable about leaving a message:

• **Update your personal greeting regularly.**

It is best to record a new greeting on a daily basis. If you cannot do that, record a new greeting every Monday morning, letting callers know your schedule for the week.

• **Let callers know when you will return their call.**

For example, "by 5 p.m. today" or "within two hours" ... and stick to it.

• **Include information about how callers can reach a co-worker who can help them if you are not available.**

This is especially important if you are on vacation or away from the office for an extended period of time.

- **Tell your callers how they can easily reach someone "live" if their call is urgent.**

  "If you need to reach someone immediately, dial 0."

- **Make sure an operator or receptionist answers the line during standard business hours.**

  Callers transfer to your receptionist for a reason – they should not be shunted into a second voice mailbox.

- **If you will be away from the office on business or on vacation and not checking messages, let callers know and tell them how to reach a colleague who is taking your calls.**

  "This is Michael McCann. I'll be on vacation from January 15 to January 22 and will not be checking messages. While I'm away, Hillary Andrews at extension 1234 can help you."

- **Check for voice messages regularly.**

  Especially if you are out of the office and do not have a flashing light or message waiting tone to remind you.

- **Let callers know about the system.**

  Tell your regular callers your company is installing voice mail, so they are prepared to leave a message when they first reach your voice mailbox. Consider sending out mailings to customers prior to installing voice mail.

- **Answer your telephone when you are at your desk.**

  Routinely screening calls is never proper business etiquette and having a voice mailbox does not make it acceptable.

- **Use the voice mail system to send and respond to messages from others in your organization.**

  Learn to think of voice mail as an abbreviated form of e-mail or memos ... but quicker.

- **Learn how to transfer callers into someone else's mailbox, or at minimum, ring their extension.**

  When you receive a call that is meant for someone else in your company, transfer the call and stay on the line until the phone is answered.

- **Time is precious.**

  The more options the caller has to tread through, the less patient they will become. Keep your recorded instructions concise. Do not overload the caller with more than four choices in any one menu. When giving instructions or options, state the option followed by the number to press – not the reverse. For example, "If you want information on our product, press 4."

  Make yourself easily accessible.

- **Print your direct telephone extension on your business card.**

  This will give your callers the option of immediately calling your number. This will create a friendly, receptive image and will make your callers feel as if they are important to you.

  Keep helping.

- **If you get a message that is not for you, do not just delete it.**

  Help the caller by forwarding their message on to the appropriate person. Preface the message with an explanation so the recipient knows why she received the voice mail.

  Alert co-workers.

- **Tell co-workers when you intend to forward your calls to their extension.**

  It is even more helpful to give them complete information about what calls you are expecting so they can be prepared to answer the caller's questions or resolve an issue.

Consider talking live.

- **When you are making a call and reach an assistant or voice mail message telling you the party is not available, ask yourself these questions to decide if your message is more appropriate for voice mail or a real person:**

How urgent is the message? How complex are the details? Will the complex message need to be passed on to others by the receiving party?

Be sensitive.

- **Be aware of topics that may be inappropriate for voice mail.**

Negative messages (such as reprimands) sound much more harsh and cold on voice mail. When speaking with someone "live," you can soften such messages with your tone, offering statements, and friendly responses to other questions.

Repeat.

- **Leave your name and phone number (with area code) at the beginning and the end of the message if it is unfamiliar to the other person.**

When people pick up their voice mail, they are often caught off guard with an unfamiliar name and number, particularly when they are said so quickly. You are more likely to get a response if you repeat your name and number at both ends of your message.

Change Your Voice Mail Greeting Frequently

True story: A customer tried for weeks to reach his sales representative. Each time he called, he heard the same voice mail message from the salesperson encouraging callers to leave a message and promising a prompt return call.

After about a month, the frustrated customer tried dialing a different extension – one number off the one he had been calling – in the hope of reaching someone. After he explained the situation to the person who picked up the phone, he was told, "Oh, you have been trying to call George? He died a month ago." Nobody had bothered to change the salesperson's voice mail.

Helpful Hints

• **Voice Mail Can Be Productive** – Many people are unduly frustrated by voice mail. Instead, adapt to this form of communication to increase your personal productivity.

• **Executives Use Voice Mail to Screen** – Decision makers routinely screen potential vendors based on the way vendors utilize voice mail.

• **Consciously Sculpt Your Voice Mail** – Keep your own voice mail messages fresh and helpful to callers.

Chapter 21

Making the Most of Your Phone Efforts

Businesspeople in America have a "love-hate" relationship with the telephone. I believe you will benefit the most in reading this chapter by my effort to combine five of my most popular articles regarding the business use of the phone. These five stories should give you a fairly complete picture on how to develop your own style to maximize your phone usage.

I. Twenty Seconds to Liftoff ...

Prospecting is something almost every businessperson hates and on which they tend to procrastinate. The telephone script is the key. Since the phone script is so critical to the prospecting success of the businessperson, let us spend time developing the script.

First, why do most professionals hate phone call prospecting? The answer I hear most often is because the perceived chance of success is so small. Many professionals have a dismal one to two percent success rate. At that rate, even strong marketers with an enormous emotional capacity for rejection will avoid telephone prospecting. It is the first thing businesspeople stop doing as soon as they get busy, causing income to go up and down like a roller coaster. Even the most seasoned businesspeople are not immune to the roller coaster. Today, with travel so expensive, businesses should make better use of the telephone. "How", you ask?

What if there was a way to increase the success rate to 50 to 70 percent? Would businesspeople scramble for telephone time? Yes, and more telephone time means a lot more potential for success.

The first thing on which we need to focus is writing a script aimed at a key decision maker. Remember that *power buys from power*. Assume for now the executive assistant transfers your call to the decision maker.

You have only a 20-second window of opportunity. The first order of business is to reduce the decision maker's anxiety over being called. I believe the primary problem professionals have with prospecting – the reason phone prospecting success rates are so low – is that businesspeople are creating *tension* rather than *interest*. How many of you have returned to your office from a long day and get a telephone call from a salesperson? It may be about telephone services, a newspaper or magazine subscription, or it may be about financial planning, whatever. Most people I know, including top-performing salespeople who should be the most tolerant of all, are intolerant of such an intrusion. From the moment they pick up the phone and hear an unfamiliar voice call them by name, their tension rises. Because of this tension, you have only 20 seconds to alleviate the tension and create interest.

Good scripting – also known as "wordsmithing" – and planning can lead you to many successful phone-prospecting calls. When creating phone scripts, here are a few things to remember:

- Make sure you can get through the script at a reasonable pace in approximately 20 seconds. That is your window of opportunity.

- Think of a problem the decision maker is *likely* to have. Do not bore the buyer with your company history. Do not ask the buyer to admit grief. Do not ask the buyer for an appointment yet.

Seek only to gain one thing: *curiosity*. Establish curiosity about how you have been able to help another person in the same situation as this decision maker, with the same job title, figure out the solution to a problem this buyer is likely to have.

Be prepared for a positive response – to continue your conversation on the phone or schedule an appointment. The foundation for a telephone prospecting script is a relevant story. It would be impossible to read most relevant stories in 20 seconds, but we do not use the entire story. We only use the predicament and important issue sections.

I believe focused, *predicament-specific* prospecting will cause a decision maker to sit up and pay attention. That is why the relevant story format starts from the base of a real predicament and an important issue. By *predicament* I mean, if I want to call doctors, I tell doctors of an *important issue* of another doctor. If I call entrepreneurs, I tell this group of another entrepreneur's important issue and how I helped that entrepreneur. If I want to call vice presidents of finance, I tell this segment how I have helped another vice president of finance solve a problem. In other words, intelligent assumptions are needed in order to put together a phone script. Intelligent assumptions focus in on a person's predicament.

Here is one example of a 20-second telephone script you can customize:

"This is (name) with (company). We have been working with (industry) for the past (number of) years. One of the chief concerns I am hearing from other (the other person's job title) is their frustration with ("wordsmithed" important issue). We have been able to help our customers deal with this issue and I would like an opportunity to share with you how."

Here is a specific example of an effective phone script targeted for the vice president of sales for a toy company.

Seller. "Tom, my name is Mike McCann with The Business Cafe™. We have been working with the toy industry for the past four years. One of the chief concerns I am hearing from other sales executives is the frustration of their salespeople not being able to reach the key decision makers at prospect companies, causing them to lose valuable sales to their competition. We have been able to help our customers deal with this issue and I would like an opportunity to share with you how."

Buyer. "Tell me more."

That script does exactly what I want. Tom, the prospect, responds with, "Tell me more." That is *curiosity*.

My customers confirm that when their phone scripts are crafted well, they get spectacular results. Such scripts have to be wordsmithed and practiced. No extra "uhs" or "ums." Each telephone script has to be smooth and tight. I have customers who report up to 80 percent curiosity rate. That means 80 percent of the time they are hearing, "Tell me more." The key is the important issue and how you wordsmith the important issue. Put some anxiety in it. Accent the *frustration* you are hearing from the decision maker's peers.

Here is a shorter but still effective phone script that I can use with the CEO of a computer hardware company:

"Mr. Jones, my name is Mike McCann. I write in-house newsletters for computer companies. Some of my customers include the ABC Company and the XYZ Company. One of the chief concerns I am hearing from other marketing communication directors is their frustration over the inability to communicate the same message to all their employees in a timely manner. I have been able to help my customers deal with this issue, and I'd like an opportunity to share with you how."

In 20 seconds with this phone script, a businessperson is asking a decision maker, are *you* curious how someone with *your* job title in *your* industry has already figured out how to solve a problem that *you* might also have? That is one of the secrets to developing new business.

When I prepare a phone script, I like to start with four important issues. I pick the one that is most probable for the initial script. Then I have the others in reserve. Why? As you may have already figured out, decision makers do not always say, "Tell me more." Sometimes they say, "I don't have that problem." So I can then say, "Other problems I have also helped our customers deal with are (important issues B, C, and D). Are you curious how I have helped our customers deal with those issues?" Now it is down to a "yes" or a "no". If it is a "no", say, "Thank you for your time" and move on to the next phone call.

This is your job in business development. To go through your conceptual target markets and turn latent need into active need. When your prospect is curious, it is the beginning of the buying cycle. If you are the businessperson who initiates the buying cycle, your competition will have to compare their products and services to the buyer's vision created by you.

If, after your best efforts, the answer is still "no", and you had to say, "Thank you for your time," you have done your job. Very little time and effort was placed with this prospect, no travel expenses were wasted and no costly demonstrations were employed.

Ask yourself, if a prospect is not curious about how you helped someone with the *same* job title at another company in the *same* industry with four important issues related to their predicament, would that have been a tough sales call had you gone out in person? Another possibility when you phone is that you get delegated down a level. If you do, you will have a much easier time getting access to key decision makers then if you begin low. Most businesspeople have had the experience of getting "locked in" at a low level in an organization. By calling high, you can avoid this problem. If you call high, the "important issue" and conversation must be *appropriate* for that level. If you find yourself getting delegated on a regular basis, you might be talking to a high-level buyer about low-level issues.

Many businesspeople admit to me that there are not enough active prospects in their sales funnel for them to achieve their goals. I poll my prospect universe twice a year to find interested buyers. When I discover one, I phone high and get delegated down to the correct decision maker. I then attempt to redesign the existing vision and qualify the buying process.

Most of our target market, though, is that huge *latent needs* area. The advantage here is, if you are first, you will get to write the buying requirements. And if you continue to challenge your prospects with further anxiety questions and further visions every time you talk with them, your buyer will "see it" a little more each time. Yes, they will look at other alternatives. That is the way corporations buy. But no other competitor can easily march in and take that buyer from you.

What if you are in a situation where your business, product, service or idea is new? If the foundation of a good phone script is a good relevant story, what do you do? One of the big secrets to prospecting still applies. It is still possible to ask buyers the question, *are you curious?* Here is an example.

Caller. "Dave, this is Michael McCann and I am with the The Business Cafe™. For the past four years, we have been doing research into the operational problems of toy companies. A problem I encounter again and again is their difficulty filling many of the orders taken by their field salespeople. We have developed a new approach to deal with this challenge, and I would like the opportunity to share with you how we have begun to help the toy industry deal with this issue."

What makes it go? The important issue. If your buyer becomes curious about how somebody has figured out how to solve their problem, they will see you. They will say, "Tell me more." The keys are the important issue and curiosity. Are they curious how someone has solved a problem?

I encourage my customers to keep success rate statistics. You might discover that only half the time with important issue "A" you get interest, but you get curiosity 80 percent of the time with important issue "B". Your success rates will vary by predicament and by important issue. I had a customer who was experimenting with different versions of a phone script. They found that by changing *one* word in a phone script, the success rate went from 40 percent to 80 percent. Try many approaches, many scripts, and keep statistics.

The Business Cafe™ telephone script is a proven way to dramatically reduce the rejection of traditional prospecting. The "are you curious?" theme can be carried to a number of other prospecting areas: Direct mail, seminars, and trade shows.

II. Four Keys to Getting Appointments by Phone

Your telephone can be a highly effective tool for qualifying prospects and confirming appointments. Strengthening your telephone skills can help boost your success rate every time you pick up the phone.

Hancock Information Group (Longwood, FL), a business-to-business telemarketing firm specializing in high-tech, high-ticket telemarketing, has pooled the collective knowledge of a group of 10 of their best telemarketers. These experts concentrate on setting qualified appointments for their customers who sell computer hardware and software, notes president Susan Hancock. "The average unit of sale is $100,000," she reports, "and some sales are in the million-dollar category."

Hancock's telemarketers are persuading senior-level executives on the merits of reserving time to listen to a sales presentation. To be successful, telemarketers must have extensive product knowledge. Their real level of expertise lies in reaching and qualifying senior-level decision makers.

You are most likely using the telephone to set up appointments for yourself rather than others. The skills are basically the same. The following tips can help ensure that you get the opportunity to speak with people who can make buying decisions.

Know Your Products and Services

"Our people know about mainframes, client servers, personal computers, software, operating systems and the correct terminology," says Hancock. "We work for many different companies and are routinely exposed to new information from our customers, so our learning curve is pretty quick. A person learns how to learn," she asserts.

Whether you are representing one company or are manufacturer's agents selling for several firms, strong product knowledge is crucial to getting appointments with potential buyers. How do you fit increasing your product knowledge into your busy day? A little bit of learning can add up to a lot. For example, if you devote only 20 minutes a week to this task, you will have spent 8½ hours every 6 months increasing your product knowledge.

Fine-Tune Your Conversational Skills

Hancock telemarketers are furnished with a script that contains specific qualifying questions, Susan explains. "If we have a product that is valuable to a mainframe user, for example, we want to be sure that the prospect company uses mainframes." Salespeople do not sell by script alone. "We want our representatives to use their own intelligence and use a conversational approach," she adds. "Once you have qualified your prospect, focus your conversation on the purpose of your call," Hancock advises. "Talk about features and benefits. Don't forget to ask for the appointment – every time," she stresses. "You won't get the appointment unless you ask for it."

... Not a social setting. The conversational techniques you will use in your phone calls are not the same as you would use in a social setting. Do not linger on discussions about the weather, sports, and the like. Instead, generate interest for your proposal through focused conversation and questioning. Once you have piqued the prospect's interest, Hancock's telemarketers set the appointment.

Overcome Objections

The professionals at Hancock do not accept a refusal the first time prospects say they are not interested – and neither should you. "The objective at this point is to determine whether the prospect truly has no interest or simply says "no" to anyone he or she perceives to be a salesperson," says Hancock. "Follow the prospect's initial refusal with something like 'Oh, I understand. Just for my records, would you mind if I asked you a couple of quick questions?' or 'Oh, you're not interested. So you have heard of our company (or my product/service)?'"

It is not easy to hear "no" and continue the conversation. That is a hallmark of a true professional. Being prepared with responses to common objections will make it easier for you to continue. Remember to empathize first – and then proceed.

Treat Secretaries and Assistants as Allies

Sometimes you have to sell a secretary or an assistant before you have access to the prospect.

Hancock's experts agree. Here are five of their suggestions:

1. "Be persistent and polite, but firm."
2. "Learn and use the secretary's/assistant's name."
3. "Earn the person's respect."
4. "Convey a sense of urgency and the belief that what you're doing is important."
5. "If you're asked a question, respond appropriately. Then follow up with your own question."

Do not think of the secretary or assistant as someone who blocks your access to the prospect. Think of this person as an ally. Once you do, you will find it easier to ask, "What do I have to do to get your boss to take my call?"

Is it harder to do business these days? Not in Hancock's opinion. "I think people are basically in business to buy and sell products," she says. "They have to buy products to deliver products to their customers." Prospects probably have less time and do not sit and have coffee with all vendors, but that can be a positive thing. "When prospects make an appointment to see you," Hancock points out, "they're sincerely interested in hearing about what you have to sell."

III. Seven Phone Marketing Traps and How to Avoid Them

Behind the anonymity of the telephone, your sales prospect operates with a hidden agenda. Often, the prospect does not want to buy but does not like to say "no" either.

The prospect sets traps for the unwary marketer, sometimes inadvertently, sometimes on purpose. Everything from "Let me think it over" to "I do business with my brother-in-law" to "Business is lousy and we don't have any money."

Here are seven traps every phone-based marketer has faced and some responses that keep prospects talking. They may actually turn a "no" into a "maybe" and a "maybe" into a "yes."

1. **"Send me more information."**

You may consider this a positive expression of interest. More likely, it is a way to end the conversation.

The best response to this trap is, "I'd be delighted. Let us be sure that I send you information that is really meaningful to you. May we spend a few minutes exploring what you're most interested in so I'll know exactly what to send?"

Then add, "I'm going to put a bright label on the envelope that says the things we talked about are inside. I only ask in return that we have a conversation a week from now to discuss the material."

2. **"Just send the information and if I'm interested, I'll call you."**

That answer is a big yellow caution flag. The person has lowered his or her value as a prospect saying, in effect, "I don't want to have a follow-up conversation."

If the customer is not willing to converse later, send a one-page letter and your FACT page in a 37-cent envelope or use First-class stamps instead of your complete fulfillment package.

3. **"We need a demonstration/evaluation copy." (for software marketers).**

This is a high-tech version of "Send me more information." Unsophisticated marketers think there must be real interest, since they want to try the program out. More likely, when the box arrives, it sits on somebody's desk because there is no compelling reason to try it.

Your answer: "If you were to evaluate it, what aspects would attract your greatest attention?" If they do not know, do not send the demonstration disk just yet. Send printed literature instead.

4. **"Sounds great! When are you coming to see me?"**

In these days of the $400-plus sales call, that is a trap (and a very expensive one, too). Response: "We can usually accomplish everything right here on the phone. Will that be OK?"

If the prospect insists on a personal visit, ask what happens next. Who will be there? Write down the names of the participants, their roles, and prerogatives. Turn a routine demonstration into an event. Do a careful ROI (return on investment) analysis. Go only if necessary. After all, your job is not to make trips, but to sell on the phone.

5. **"I have to discuss this with other people."**

    "Tell me about the other people. Who does what in the decision process? Tell me about your timetables." Get the whole story! Pin the prospect down.

6. **"It's not in our budget."**

    The response to that comment is to learn whether this purchase is ordinary but off-cycle. "Does that mean there's no budget now, not ever, or is it a nice idea whose time hasn't come?" When will a purchase like this come up for consideration? Is a supplemental appropriation possible?

7. **"You're a fabulous salesperson, but ..."**

    This is not a compliment. "It is a "put-down!" The prospect is saying that you have described product features rather than asked the right questions. You may have made a benefit statement without knowing how the product or service will be used. In other words, told about the product or service but not sold on the product or service. In these days of corporate "right-sizing", a lot of responsibility – but not authority – has shifted downward. Prospects may bring you along in good faith without realizing they cannot make the decision. To avoid embarrassment, they stall and invent excuses.

    Recognize this new state of business life. Ask questions but do not press. Give the prospect a face saving way out. When that person goes up the ladder and gets the authority, you will have made a good friend and long-term customer.

IV. Five Quirks That Irk Customers on the Phone

Although you think you are doing everything possible to sound courteous and professional to callers, you can unknowingly display a habit or mannerism that offends the person on the other end of the phone.

Here are five common ways businesspeople antagonize the person on the other end of the phone conversation and what you can do about them.

1. **Talk too fast.**

People in business receive so many calls they may unintentionally speak quickly to hurry the call along.

If this is your quirk: Slow down your pace! People generally speak at an average speed of 126 words per minute. Time yourself to see where your average falls and strike a natural pace.

2. **Hang up too quickly.**

In their zeal to get to the next call quickly, businesspeople sometimes hang up before the other person is ready.

If this is your quirk: "Remember, call beginnings and call endings are like bookends," says Chicago-based consultant Lisa Shurer. "They support the rest of the call. A friendly closing tells the other person, 'We've conducted business, and maybe even disagreed, but, in the end, we are friendly, and we respect one another.' People are social creatures, and we need that kind of affirmation." Call endings need not be lengthy or complicated: A simple pleasantry like, "It was nice talking with you" will end the call on a positive note.

3. **Sound too casual.**

Businesspeople who do not use language effectively sometimes clutter their speech with phrases such as "you know," "like," and "uh."

If this is your quirk: Record your side of a phone conversation and play it back later, suggests Peter Guiliano, President of the Executive Communication Group, Inc. "Then force yourself to stop using the junk words and phrases that bring down the quality of your presentation."

4. **Sound distracted.**

Other customers, phone calls, or even co-workers can distract you while you are on the phone. If you let distractions grab your attention, however, customers will pick up on it very quickly.

If this is your quirk: Do not fake it. If another concern is so pressing that it cannot be put aside, quickly explain the situation, put the conversation on hold, take care of the concern, and then return to pay undivided attention to the customer.

5. **Sound exhausted.**

After a long day of busy phones and difficult phone calls, you can have difficulty keeping the oomph! in your phone manners.

If this is your quirk: Close your eyes and visualize. "This approach at first may seem unorthodox," admits Thomas McCafferty, director of production for Houston-based TeleCross Corporation. "But based on my experience, it works."

Here is what to do: Before taking your next call, close your eyes. Breathe slowly and deeply. Imagine that the phone rings and you have answered it smiling and full of energy and enthusiasm. Take another long breath. Now reach for the phone.

V. Phone Habits That Keep Harmony at Work

When you work in close quarters with several others, it is all too easy to crisscross each other with bad telephone behavior. Reduce this risk by following these seven thoughtful telephone habits.

• **Modulate your telephone voice.**

Keep in mind that you are not working in a private environment. People all around you are trying to work – and they cannot do that amid loud conversations and raucous laughter. Keep your voice as low as you can while still sounding natural and friendly to the caller.

- **Answer your ringing telephone as quickly as possible.**

Pick up by the third ring – but sooner is best. A phone that keeps ringing is stressful to co-workers. This stress level increases when several phones in the work area ring excessively.

- **Observe the rules of etiquette for using portable phones.**

Most important, be unobtrusive. Remember the last time you were in a meeting or at a social function where a cell phone user seemed oblivious to everyone else around him or her? Annoying, wasn't it? Turn your phone off in a meeting. When you take a break from the meeting, you can check for, and try to return, voice messages quickly.

- **Keep personal calls to a minimum.**

Talking on company time with family and friends is cheating, but it also distracts your co-workers. Not only that, it can keep you from meeting your work commitments as well.

Follow company policy on personal calls. Make as few personal calls as possible. Ask family and friends to call you at work only in an emergency.

- **Use the "call forwarding" feature on your telephone system when you are unable to take calls.**

Forwarding your phone will not bother others with repeated ringing when you are not there. If you do not have call forwarding, alert co-workers when you are expecting a call but must be away from your desk. Provide any information they need to deal with the caller. That could include an alternate number where you are at the moment, or a time when you will be back at your desk to return the call.

- **Be professional when taking calls and messages for others.**

  Write the message while you are speaking with the caller. If you wait until later, you may forget key points. Be sure to get the correct name, telephone number, and best time to return the call. Be courteous, friendly, and helpful as you would be with the individual you respect most in the world.

- **Spare others your work-related stress.**

  Do not slam down the receiver out of frustration after dealing with a particularly challenging phone call. Deal with your stress in other, more productive ways, such as meditating, or taking a brisk walk down the hall at break time.

One of the biggest mistakes you can make on the phone is not warming up your voice before participating in a call. It takes two hours for your voice to warm up, so if you have an important call at 9 a.m., wake up at 7 a.m. and make noises in the shower to get the frog out of your throat. If you have not talked much during the day, your voice gets rusty. Before making a critical or long call, loosen up your pitch and modulation by chatting with a friend or colleague.

What is the first thing you should do when the phone rings? Take a deep breath and smile. You never know when it is a potential customer with a large order calling. Always use the same greeting because it becomes your brand.

What makes a voice sound confident? First, never lie to a customer, even if you do not know the answer to a question. A lying or nervous voice comes across either as monotone, clipped, or too high. The biggest pitfall is when customers ask about price. If you charge $150 an hour and a customer says, "That's a lot of money," say, "Yes, it is," clearly and with confidence.

Helpful Hints

- **Make the Phone Your Ally** – Plan detailed, well-timed scripts and responses before calling prospect number one.

- **Know Your Products and Services** – When you are on the phone with a decision maker, you have no time to "think" about responses to product and service questions ... you have to know the information "cold".

- **Develop a Conversational Tone** – Once you are confident with knowing all you can know about your products, services and company, relax on the phone and try to help the prospect or customer solve their problem.

- **Guard Against Being Too "Soft"** – If a prospect or customer is trying, in subtle or not-so-subtle means, to be quick with you on the phone, propose that your timing or offering may not be appropriate and come back to this prospect or customer another time.

- **Constantly Strive to Improve Your Phone Style** – Keep current with techniques for effective telephone usage ... your pocketbook and manager will be glad you do.

About Your Author

Michael McCann is Managing Director of The Business Café, a full-service business development company. Michael speaks before associations and companies about business development topics and develops customized business development programs for customers worldwide.

Mr. McCann writes for magazines, newsletters and Web sites. Two of his most popular titles include, *Reaching the Key Decision Maker* and *Arrogance in the Workplace*. Many people refer to Michael's writing as a humorous touch to serious themes.

Mr. McCann publishes ***E-lert*™**, a fortnightly Webletter. Each issue is designed for people interested in growing their business and succeeding in spite of office politics, available by subscribing at www.BusinessCafeOnline.com.

"I am often asked my advice in developing a business development program for a specific association or company. No two associations or companies are the same. There is no business development template ... every organization needs a unique plan for developing long-term business," Mike says.

In order to answer your specific questions about developing your own business development program and make recommendations that fit your organization "like a glove"; we need a face-to-face meeting. Face-to-face initial meetings are complimentary and here are the details:

• Meeting face-to-face at your organization's office prior to lunch for review of current business practices and what you wish to accomplish with a business development program. Your organization will be obligated only for my customary travel expenses.

- You choose the individuals in your organization you wish to include in our meeting and you treat the group to lunch.

- At the conclusion of lunch, I will give you and your group specific information towards constructing a business development program that I believe will be most effective for what I've heard, seen and studied about your organization.

- You, and your colleagues, decide whether or not you wish to retain my services with all the details laid out at that time.

I've spelled it all out here. No surprises and very little time and money investment on your part to see if you want to pursue a comprehensive business development program, or what you have in place is working the best.

If you want to discuss specifics, call 800-335-8161 or e-mail me at:

Mike@BusinessCafeOnline.com

Prior to working in business development, writing and speaking, Michael was a salesperson in Dallas and southern California where he developed the first programs for reaching the key decision maker. In 1997, Michael produced an innovative audio/Internet program illustrating more than eleven methods for business development that have consistently proven successful.

Michael founded Com*Perfect Systems, a successful direct mail marketing facility in southern California in 1985, and sold the business for a profit in 1989. Later that same year, he founded Postmark USA, a nationwide telephone headset distributorship and repair facility in central Texas. In 1994, Michael sold the headset company and has been Managing Director of The Business Café ever since.

A graduate of Baylor University with a Marketing degree, Mr. McCann also earned an MBA from Texas A&M-Corpus Christi. He grew up in Corpus Christi, Texas, and lived in southern California before moving to Austin, Texas, in 1989. Michael has also lived in Columbus, Ohio, and St. Thomas, U.S.V.I., before moving to Raleigh, North Carolina.

Order Form

⌐───┐

- Fax orders: (800) 557-2656
- Phone orders: call Toll Free: (800) 335-8161, Have your MasterCard or VISA ready.
- Online orders: www.BusinessCafeOnline.com
- Postal Orders: Cheryl Elliott
                          The Business Café™
                          5948 Dunbarton Way
                          Raleigh, NC 27613-6856
                          Telephone: (800) 335-8161
                          Mike@BusinessCafeOnline.com

I understand that I may return books for a full refund – for any reason, no questions asked within 30 days.

⌐───┐

☐ Please send **Connecting With Key Decision Makers** for only $16.95 each (quantity discounts for more than 10 at one time) to:

Company name: _____

Name: _____

Address: _____

City: _____ State: _____ Postal: _____

Telephone: (_____) _____

Sales tax:
Please add 7.00% for books shipped to North Carolina addresses.

Shipping:
$3.95 for the first book and $2.00 for each additional book.

Payment:
☐ Check ☐ VISA, ☐ MasterCard Exp. Date: _____ / _____

Card Number: _____

Name on card: _____

Signature: _____

Order today, you will be glad tomorrow.

Appendix

Information Marketing Services
8130 Boone Boulevard, # 320
Vienna, VA 22182
703-821-8130
www.greatlists.com

Guide to International Mailing Lists
Lists 600 International business-to-business mailing lists

InfoUSA, Inc.
5711 S. 86th Circle
P.O. Box 27347
Omaha, NE 68127-0347
800-321-0869
www.InfoUsa.com

Mailing List Compiler

American List Counsel, Inc.
4300 Route 1
CN 5219
Princeton, NJ 08543
800-ALC-LIST
www.amlist.com

Mailing List Compiler

Kroll Direct Marketing
101 Morgan Lane, Suite 120
Plainsboro, NJ 08536
609-275-2900
www.krolldirect.com

Mailing List Compiler

Dunhill Int'l List Co., Inc.
1951 NW 19th Street
Boca Raton, FL 33431-7344
800-DUNHILL
www.dunhills.com

Mailing List Compiler

PCS Mailing List Company
39 Cross Street
Peabody, MA 01960-1628
800-532-5478
www.pcslist.com

Mailing List Compiler

Dun & Bradstreet Information
103 JFK Parkway
Short Hills, NJ 07078
973-921-5500
www.dnb.com

Mailing List company

Omnigraphics
615 Griswold
Detroit, MI 48226
313-961-1340
www.omnigraphics.com

Toll-Free Phone Book
US toll free numbers for
businesses

Hoovers, Inc.
5800 Airport Boulevard
Austin, Texas 78752
512-374-4500
www.hoovers.com

Excellent business
directories

U.S. Demography Home Page
www.ciesin.org/datasets/us-demog/us-demog-home.html
contains links to almost every major statistic and
demographic resource on the Web

Japs-Olson
7500 Excelsior Boulevard
St. Louis Park, MN 55426
952-932-9393
www.japsolson.com

Commercial Printing

Spencer Press, Inc.
90 Spencer Drive
Wells, ME 04090
207-646-9926
www.spencerpress.com

Commercial Printing

U.S. Press, Inc.
1628 James P. Rodgers Drive
Valdosta, GA 31601
800-227-7377
www.uspress.com

4-color postcards,
brochures

United Micro Printing
19355 Business Center Dr, # 3
Northridge, CA 91324
888-774-6889
www.UnitedMicroPrinting.com

4-color flyers, brochures

Tu-Vets Printing
5635 E. Beverly Boulevard
Los Angeles, CA 90022
800-894-8977
www.tu-vets.com

4-color flyers

Paper Direct Internet
1025 East Woodmen Road
Colorado Springs, CO 80920
800-A-Papers
www.paperdirect..com

Business stationery

Hallmark Business Expressions
P.O. Box 419034
Kansas City, MO 64141
800-404-0081
www.hallmarkbusiness.com

Business-to-business
card catalog

New Pueblo Enterprises
660 South Country Club
Tucson, AZ 85716
800-546-6556
(no Web site as of July 2003)

Phoney Greeting Cards

Getty Images Creative
2013 Fourth Avenue
Seattle, WA 98121
877-438-8966
http://creative.gettyimages.com/p
hotodisc

Excellent for
photographs/images

Rapidocolor
705 East Union Street
West Chester, PA 19382
800-872-7436
www.rapidocolor.com

Short to long runs of color
collateral

Champion Printing, Inc.
575 Murphy Drive
Jackson, MI 49202
800-526-1135
http://www.championprinting.net/

Excellent source for direct
mail piece production

The American Stationery Co.   Personalized stationery
300 North Park Avenue
Peru, IN 46970
800-822-2577
www.AmericanStationery.com

Maximizer   Contact Manager
1090 W. Pender St., 10th Floor   software
Vancouver, B.C. V6E 2N7
604-601-8000
www.maximizer.com

Interact Commerce   Act! contact software
8800 N. Gainey Center Dr., #200   SalesLogix is Customer
Scottsdale, AZ 85258   Relationship
480-368-3700   Management (CRM)
www.act.com   software for
www.saleslogix.com   small to mid-sized
          companies

FrontRange Solutions, Inc.   GoldMine contact
1125 Kelly Johnson Boulevard   software
Colorado Springs, CO 80920
800-776-7889
www.frontrange.com

Group 1 Software   PC to mainframe contact
4200 Parliament Place, # 600   software
Lanham, MD 20706-1844
888-413-6763
www.g1.com

Wally Amos Snacks   Chocolate Chip cookies
P.O. Box 897   and muffins
Kailua, HI 96734   ("Famous Amos")
808-261-6075
www.wallyamos.com
www.auntdellascookies.com

PC/Nametag   Source for name badges
124 Horizon Drive   and nametags
Verona, WI 53593
877-626-3824
www.pcnametag.com

Trade Show Exhibitors Assoc.
McCormick Place
2301 S. Lake Shore Dr., # 1005
Chicago, IL 60616
312-842-8732
www.tsea.org

Exhibit and Event
Marketing
Professionals

OnContact Software Corporation
W67 N222 Evergreen Blvd.-#212
Cedarburg, WI 53012
262-375-6555
www.oncontact.com

Customer Relationship
Management
(CRM) software for mid-
market companies

Disc Makers
7905 N. Route 130
Pennsauken, NJ 08110-1402
856-663-9030
www.discmakers.com

CD and DVD machines
and supplies

Index

setting up your own, 218-221
time zones, 217
Voice Messaging Educational
Committee, 218
volleyball, 99
VOLTS, 84

Y

Yahoo, 145

W

Wall Street Journal, 13
water, 75, 100
Waterford Crystal, 96
web presentations software,
149
Webcasting, 150-151
Services, 150
Software, 150
webchat, 144
WebInnovation, 85
Web sites
content, 142-143
designing for women, 151
home page, 145
information-based sites, 82
linking, 145-146
strategic alliances, 153
transaction-based sites, 83
with voice mail, 142, 144
WinFAX Pro, 161
*World's Best-Known Marketing
Secret,* 28
Writing
from other person's point-of-
view, 164

Printed in the United States
18961LVS00001B/209

9 780741 414946